BIG BLACK PENIS

MISADVENTURES IN **RACE** AND **MASCULINITY**

SHAWN TAYLOR

Lawrence Hill Books

Library of Congress Cataloging-in-Publication Data
Taylor, Shawn.
  Big black penis : misadventures in race and masculinity / Shawn
Taylor.
     p. cm.
  ISBN-13: 978-1-55652-734-0
  ISBN-10: 1-55652-734-9
  1. African American men—Race identity. 2. African American men—
Social conditions. 3. African American men—Psychology. 4.
Masculinity—United States. 5. Penis—Social aspects—United States. 6.
Taylor, Shawn. I. Title.

  E185.625T394 2008
  305.38'896073—dc22

                              2007038697

For my wife and our ancestors.

Cover and interior design: Jonathan Hahn
Cover photograph: Tetsunori Ishida

Published in 2008 by Lawrence Hill Books
An imprint of Chicago Review Press, Incorporated
814 North Franklin Street
Chicago, Illinois 60610
ISBN 978-1-55652-734-0
Printed in the United States of America
5 4 3 2 1

Contents

Introduction

This book is not some navel-gazing attempt to publicly emasculate myself in order to garner female understanding and sympathy in hopes of getting laid. I'm married—I already have a beautiful woman to have sex with. I wrote this book because it was necessary.

I'm just a regular cat, but I felt a need to throw down my gauntlet on the battlefield of masculine discourse. Going through the bookstores and trying to find anything resembling a men's studies section was disheartening. The books were few, overwhelmingly white, written for an older generation, or—to my utter surprise—written by women. Nothing applied to me, so I thought I'd add my take.

Over the years, I have tackled the subject of masculinity in several other formats—spoken word and slam poetry. I even produced a couple of highly successful, albeit locally performed and attended, solo theatrical performances, *Doing Time at the Front Door*, my account of being a bouncer at a popular nightclub, and *Man Versus Hood*, basically a rant against my father, poverty, and my mother's emotional distance. But I felt that these weren't effective enough.

It seemed the right time for a dude—like myself—to document what I need to say about myself instead of letting others do the talking for me. I have no illusion that my work will usher in a new wave of positive masculine consciousness. But I do believe that the reader will gain some insight into the complexities of black masculine culture. If you get one thing from this book, I hope it is the understanding that this culture is not monolithic. Each of its facets should be taken as a valid and legitimate expression of a full life as opposed to an aberration. We are as different and varied as any other culture.

Even though Wesley Snipes and Alan Keyes are roughly the same color, I doubt they'll be sharing chicken and cognac anytime soon. Danny Glover and Ward Connerly probably aren't planning to play dominoes next Saturday night. Get the picture?

To all of my brothers from other races, cultures, and creeds, I apologize for not including you in my book. I did not feel qualified to do so. If you feel slighted in any way, do what I did: somehow, anyhow, get your voice out there. If you don't, some asshole from some news station or marketing department or BET or MTV will do it for you. Speak now or be spoken for.

Penisis

The Genesis of the Penis

I guess the whole thing started with the penis. Not the little cashew that dangled between my legs and that I peed out of, but the symbolic penis. You know, the everything-that-is-wrong-and-harmful-to-this-world-is-shaped-like-it penis. The bullet, the nuclear missile, the skyscraper, the reason that women hate men, the black man's handhold, the almighty scepter of masculinity. When I learned that a penis wasn't just an organ for pleasure, waste management, and procreation but had a whole multipage Wikipedia entry unto itself, I freaked out.

My first exposure to penis power was in the second grade, in my mythology unit. The teacher was explaining how Set chopped up Osiris and sent his various parts all over the place. Then Isis, Osiris's sister-wife, found some of his pieces, got pregnant, and gave birth to Horus. The teacher did a wonderful job of not spelling out *how* Isis got pregnant. She probably figured that we were having a hard enough time wrapping our heads around the whole *sister-wife* thing. We second-graders may not have been very well versed in the reproductive arts, but we for damn sure knew that a woman couldn't get pregnant by some nebulous body part; not even a goddess had powers like that. So, of course, we pressed her into giving us more detail. Boy, did she!

"Isis was made pregnant—um—by Osiris's—um—private parts that were found in a—stone pillar." After spitting it out, she cringed as if expecting to be fired on the spot.

The effect on the class was amazing. This is when, in my experience, the gender division began. The girls, those who understood what was said, wore either knowing smiles (with some giggling) or looks of untamed disgust. We boys covered our laps and shrank in our seats, contemplating the power of the pee-pee. After hearing that, I would never be the same. This was Defining Life Moment (DLM) #1.

I am a thirty-four-year-old man, and my penis is still a mystery to me. Don't get me wrong—I know how it works, and I am quite adept in its use (male ego chiming in). But I am still tripped out by the intense reactions people have whenever the penis is a topic of conversation. Like if I call it a "penis," most people look at me as if I had spat on their mother.

"It's not a penis, man! It's a dick!"

Then the conversation turns to something less controversial, like fistfights. This is what happens with my guy friends. My female friends, including my wife, all have little nicknames for "it." Some are cute, like "coo coo," and some are downright odd, like "Charlie Mack." I shouldn't complain too much—at least it is OK for me to speak about my penis in public. If women were this "bold," I bet that most people would either not take them seriously or think they were being sluttish. Major big ups to Eve Ensler for her *Vagina Monologues*! Do your thing! I think that genitalia, and the baggage that comes with them, should be in the public discourse at all times.

When we talk about the penis, we have to discuss the construction of a man's masculine identity. Yes, I use the word *construction* because one doesn't just become a man. The neighborhood, culture, economic status, and hosts of other things help to dictate what type of men we become. Masculinity is a construction, and just like femininity it has been co-opted, reshaped, remixed, expanded, shrunk, polluted, and diluted. The fruits of this construction look different from femininity. Men have been, and are currently, in power, and we can spin and manipulate our shit to make us look as if we're on top of it. But most of us are not as put together and confident as we appear.

I can tell you the exact moment when I saw the construction for what it was: a system of imagery and expectations designed to make me feel inferior to all other males. The year was 1985, and I was twelve years old. My friends and I went to go see that guilty pleasure of a movie *Krush Groove*. All of us were enjoying the movie, and then LL Cool J showed up. This was DLM #2.

As LL burst on the screen, his sixteen-year-old masculine energy forced everyone in the theater to lean way back. He spat those famous words:

> *Nobody can rap*
> *Quite like I can*
> *I'll take a muscle-bound man*
> *And put his face in the sand*

All any of us could say was "Whoa." After the flick, I went home, took off my shirt, and began to flex in front of the bathroom mirror. What an awful sight. You could've laid me on my back, poured water in the concavity that was supposed to be my chest, and let goldfish swim in there. I was not the man that LL was. Hell, I'd probably never be *that*. That shit looked way too hard to pull off, and I didn't yet have the skill set. At least that was what I thought back then. Later I discovered that a man could wear many shapes and could be many things. But first I still had a bunch of heartbreaking lessons to learn.

One of the biggest lessons was that my penis didn't make me superior. Now, don't think that I'm on some my-penis-makes-me-a-bad-boy emasculation shit. I'm not one of those pseudo–Million Man March brothers who feels the need to apologize for things I never did (or would do). This is not where we're going. But our society has a severe case of *the-penis-is-good* positive reinforcement syndrome. (Not the actual penis, mind you, but the phallus.)

Everywhere we men look, someone or something is telling us that our dangling bits make us kings. Just look at Hollywood. Jack Nicholson and Sean Connery, their collective ages totaling almost a century and a half, are still considered sex symbols. When an actress hits her late thirties, she is no longer sexy. More attention is focused on her acting ability than her sex appeal. And that's bullshit. But there can be only a set number of kings, and we spend most of our time trying to dethrone all pretenders to the crown—anyone and everyone who doesn't conform to our retarded, self-involved visions of masculinity. Sad, isn't it?

This bit is for the females, if any are reading this book. The next time you see an average group of men—not too Banana Republic and not too Wrangler, somewhere in the middle—sneak up close enough to eavesdrop on their conversation. If they're good friends, there is a good chance they are talking about something interesting, maybe even heartfelt. Now, wait for a hot woman to walk past and catch one of the guy's eyes. If you are that hot woman, walk by them, but do it slowly. Walk by slowly enough to hear the shift in their conversation.

One minute these friends are talking about theology, philosophy, or particle physics, but as soon as a female presence enters their orbit, someone in the group is gonna get insulted. This cat is the one the others feel isn't as *manly* as they are. And this insult usually takes the form of a gibe at his sexuality—sex and sexuality, of course, being one of the few ways men quantify their masculinity.

The vulgarity of these gibes has waned in recent years. Whereas back in the day, you may have heard something along the lines of "You no-dick-havin' motherfucker," nowadays most men have developed a certain refinement when playing the dozens. Most likely, the dozens will now sound like "You don't have any idea how to please a woman." These guys were having a regular conversation, and then, out of nowhere, these insults are launched, landing in a heap in the less manly cat's lap. This poor guy hasn't the slightest clue as to what just happened. All he knows is that his friends just went Judas on him.

The female-energy disruption lasts for moments, a minute at the most. Then the hot woman breaks orbit and goes about her business (which she was handling anyway). The conversation continues at the exact spot where it was broken off. Everyone is back to normal, as if nothing happened, except for that poor bastard whose friends just dogged him out.

If he asks them why they were taking the piss out of him, they look at him like he's a really geeky dude looking through the window at a really cool and happening party. They shake their heads and silently wonder why their friend doesn't get it. Awkward silence petrifies the group like superglue, freezing everyone. One of the guys, the one all of the girls flock to and considered the coolest of the crew but actually the biggest asshole, cracks a dirty or semi-dirty joke, and everyone busts up laughing—all is back to normal. That is, until the next hot woman walks by.

You think I just pulled this out of my ass? Let me tell you true: I was that guy who was negatively baptized by the insults. Believe me, things may have superficially gone back to normal, but we, the insulted, never forget.

We don't gunnysack all of these slights to exact our revenge, although that does come into play in some cases. We hold them in to provide ammo for our auto-assault on our self-esteem. Most men, and I am wholeheartedly including myself among this number, are born to undo themselves. It may not be obvious, but men have the same esteem problems privately that women have publicly—we just don't have as many magazines, talk shows, and self-help groups constantly reminding us of them. Every man, despite the public face he presents, hates one or more things about himself.

He may be going bald early, he isn't the bedroom king he imagines himself to be, he isn't as educated as his partner, he sports some love handles or a big old sloppy gut—I could go on and on, but you get the idea. Instead of working on the areas that we hate, most of us would rather just wallow in them.

Most regular guys wear their sloppy guts like some badge of honor. They strut around, using their stomachs as a shield or a battering ram, seemingly content with where they're at and how they look. While some genetic dispositions may be involved, a lot of these cats are lazy as fuck. They have given up. Society tells them it is OK to be sloppy and unkempt, so they revel in it. The funny thing is that most of them want a thin, well-built woman to put their ham hocks on. They figure that with a thin woman in their mitts, people won't think bad of them.

"Hey, look at that guy! He's as big as two Rosie O'Donnells, but his girl is fit. He must be doing *something* right."

These poor bastards coast through life being validated by the world at large. They never do anything to combat their weight (esteem) problems. Most men in this situation do something that I like to call *The Slide*. The Slide is a doubled-edged self-defense technique that men use to become a type.

The fat dude becomes more jovial, always smiling and laughing with people, putting them at ease. He's in pain, but because he's large, he feels that he has to slide into the Santa Claus role. I don't mean to attack "weight-challenged" people. I have had my own issues with weight and am pulling from my own experience.

The Slide can easily be applied to other types of men. Let's take the man who fancies himself a *Casanova*. Pussy, pussy, pussy is all the guy thinks about. "All I'm doing is giving these women pleasure! They know what they are getting into when we hook up. It's just sex. Just beautiful sex," he spouts. This cat says it in such a poetic way that he almost convinces himself of its truth.

Let a few years of this fastest-dick-in-the-West mentality go by, and see how many damaged and irreparable relationships and people he has left trailing behind him. And Casanova is the most damaged of them all.

You've seen those miserable ex-lotharios. Everything on them is manicured to the fullest, the clothes are just right, the hair is perfect, and the car is the latest and greatest. They are usually funny and willing to do anything at a moment's notice, but they have no real personality.

"I'm coming to get you right now! We're going to Vegas. There will be women everywhere. Vegas pussy is the best, man. Pack your shit; I'm on my way."

He almost has you ready to drop everything, and then you realize that every time you are with him, you have a shitty time. It starts out great, but by the third or fourth hour, you want to put two hungry rats in a bag and put it over his head. He's miserable, and you become so, via proximity to him.

He'll go through women like he goes through pairs of socks, but he's never satisfied. It's as if he is (cliché as it sounds) trying to fill a hole that cannot be filled. With dull eyes and an army of well-worn patter, he ambles about the earth nailing anything that moves. For every dick-thrust, he appears to lose a year of his life, but he'll be damned if he will ever tell you how he's feeling. Real men don't do things like that. They "suck it up" and force others to unconsciously participate in their misery. But as long as he is fucking, he thinks, what the hell, right?

While there are still a few Casanovas out there, they are slowly being replaced by another Slide type: *the Sensitive Artist Dude (SAD).*

This type sprang up at around the same time that slam poetry and open mics and coffeehouses started to become way too popular.

Not to put this solely at one brother's feet, but the multi-hyphenate, spoken-word dervish Saul Williams is partially at fault. I'm sure he had no idea just how far his influence would reach, but now there are Saul clones running around in art scenes all over the world. This incredibly talented brother has changed his presentation, has expanded beyond his own boundaries, but his clones, the thieves of his artistic legacy, have not. They're still stuck in what this cat was doing five years ago. Fellas, it's time to lay that shit to rest.

Long before Kanye rocked button-ups, cafe poetry dudes were sporting them with the cuffs unbuttoned, paired with tattered jeans or Africanesque fabric trousers. Egyptian musk oil pouring from their bodies, they put flower petals in their pants instead of wearing underwear, and they rocked the mic, professing just how vulnerable they were. You see, vulnerability was the ace weapon of the SAD. Vulnerability is an aphrodisiac to the scores of women who attend poetry and other artistic functions. "Oh, he is so lonely and vulnerable, maybe some good sex will help him to heal." And believe me, if you are a SAD, you can have as much sex as you want. On the flip side, these cats have the most demons.

SADs know they are manipulative, but they don't have any idea how to curb their behavior. They truly think they are doing the right thing by speaking in meta-cosmic terms and comparing everything to a celestial body, but they aren't being honest with themselves. Instead of working through their pain in private, they do it among the masses in order to receive public validation for their pain. The more applause they receive, they more they pick at their emotional scabs in order to "create more art."

It is a nasty little feedback loop of bared pain, acceptance and validation of the pain, and baring more pain in order for it to be validated and accepted once again. SADs have been around for centuries in many guises and in many different cultures, but now it's my brothers' turn to adopt the mantle, and most of us are putting our SAD ancestors to shame.

All this doesn't just come out of nowhere. These are a series of steps that many men climb in order to escape the shadows of their fathers. A man's foundation should be his interaction with his father, but for so many black men, there wasn't one. Men learn how to be men by observing their fathers being men. And our fathers should have been around. Mine wasn't, and his absence left a big impact.

Daddy
Complex

I was born in 1972, post–civil rights struggle, post–Black Power movement, right smack at the dawn of the disco era. All of those black and brown fists that were once raised in defiance, raised in unity, dropped and formed a barrier between fathers and their families when I was born. The exit conversation usually went like this:

"Pregnant? I thought you said you were on the Pill. I ain't tryin' to have no kids, bitch. Look, I'll shoot you some bread from time to time, but I can't have no kids. I'm trying to get my head together." Then he would snort a couple herculean lines of coke.

And just like that, like so many black and brown children of the seventies, I was left fatherless. Fathers were a myth where I grew up, a legend kind of like the boogeyman, a tale used to straighten out crooked kids. The word *daddy* was the ultimate manipulative tool used by project mothers everywhere.

"If you don't clean up your room, I'm gonna tell your daddy not to take your ungrateful ass to the circus!"

Upon hearing that, you'd rush to your room at top speed. Like Irona from *Richie Rich*, you'd quickly and mechanically put your dirty clothes in the hamper, make your bed, and put all of your toys in their proper places. When your room was at its best, you'd rush outside and wait for your father to arrive. And you'd wait. You'd wait some more, hours, until your mother came outside and put her arm around your shoulders.

"He's not coming today, is he, Mommy?" you'd say to her, hoping that you were wrong.

"No, I don't think that he is," she'd say, without looking you in the eye.

After a couple more minutes, both of you go back inside. As you enter, you realize that you have an enormous lump in your throat, and you want to cry so badly, but you can't. For as long as you can remember, the hard rocks in your neighborhood have said that real men don't cry, so you choke back the tears.

You return to your bedroom and begin to either punch your pillow or break some toys or both. Your mother's voice cuts through your anger and disappointment.

"He shouldn't keep doing this to you."

The words bounce around for a minute, and you figure that *she* should stop doing this to you. This was the third time Daddy didn't show up, and by now you have figured out that he is never going to make an appearance. But your mother's lie feeds your hope.

I think that the Discovery Channel should have a special on absentee fathers. It would have been nice to see Steve Irwin, the Crocodile Hunter, look for black fathers. Too bad he's gone. Rest in peace. But if he were alive, his adventure would look like this:

G'day! My name is Steve Irwin, and welcome to *The Father Hunter*. Today we are in what is called the projects, and we are trying to find the most elusive creature in the entire ghetto, the father. We have to be very quiet in our search. There's one now! Shhh. Shhh. It's all right, it's OK . . . Crikey! He's fast! He must have thought we were Social Services, got frightened, and ran away. He's a very naughty boy! One thing to keep in mind, you have to be very precise in your search for the father in the ghetto because the father can easily be confused with the uncle. There are a couple of ways to tell them apart, though. You see, first off, the father only impregnates. He's only involved in the physical act. The uncle, on the other hand, plays with the child and sometimes has a hand in his or her upbringing. Till next time, g'day.

Fathers are supposed to be a boy's living instruction manual, dispensing words of wisdom and giving instructions for life. What if you have a "man" question? Who are you supposed to ask? You can't really ask your mom any questions relating to your dick.

I remember when I first got pubic hair. I was sitting on the pot when I began to itch down there. While I was scratching, much to my surprise, I felt a mini-Afro.

"Mama! Mama! Come here, quick!"

"Boy, what's with all of this noise in here?"

"Mama, look. I got hair on my peanuts!"

The look of fear on her face was so intense! "Put it away, boy. Put it away!"

This wouldn't be the last time that a woman reacted to my penis like that. To avoid embarrassment of this nature, one needs a father to provide guidance. Mothers should not have to bear that responsibility. Not to say that mothers don't have the ability or the tools to deal with this, but they shouldn't have to. The father should be around. To paraphrase an old saying: you divorce spouses, not children.

Come to think of it, aside from the pubic hair episode, almost all of my traditionally male milestones were experienced with women. One of my friend's mothers taught me to swim by tossing me into the nine-foot end of the public swimming pool. I learned to shave by practicing on a hooker's legs. Now, wait a minute. There's an innocent story behind that.

I've already informed you that my father was nowhere to be found. My mother, on the other hand, was around in the flesh, but she was about as far away emotionally from me as the moon. She had other, more pressing concerns that didn't include parenting—like inviting a host of alcoholic pugilists into our home so that they could perfect their jabs and hooks on us. With no mother—no parents—to be a son to, I kind of became a son to all of the hookers who were on the track in our neighborhood.

I'd run errands for them, buying cigarettes, booze, and mouthwash, the tools to help them get through their day. Folks in the hood used to call them all sorts of names, throw shit at them, and spit at their feet. This used to piss me off so badly because these women *cared* for me. They cared for me in a way that my mother never did; hell, maybe she wasn't even able to care for me this way. These women gave me advice, told me to stay in school, and exposed me to the horrors of life. They used their lives as examples of what not to do and who not to be like. That was an enormous, selfless gift.

One day, I was helping Marguerite, definitely a second mom to me, bring groceries up to her apartment. As we were putting away the food, she looked me dead in the face and said, "Damn, papi! You look like Grizzly Adams up in here. Haven't you ever heard of a razor?"

"Of course," I said, in my deepest, most affected voice.

"Why don't you use it then? No bitch wants a furry-ass face all up in hers. How come you don't shave?"

That threw me for a bit. Why didn't I just shave? Why was I walking around sporting a chin-and-cheek fro? The answer to my question was embarrassing. I didn't know how to shave, and that is what I told her. And to my surprise, she didn't laugh at me. She didn't even crack a smile.

"Come on. Let me show you how to do it."

We went into her bathroom, where she began to spread shaving cream up and down her right leg. She got one of those pink disposable razors from her medicine cabinet. She grabbed my hand and put it on top of hers and then began to pull the razor up her leg.

"See, you have to go against the grain of the hair. See how smooth it is? You do it like this, and your face will be just as smooth. Your turn."

The cream went on my grill, and just like with her leg, my hand over hers, we began to shave. A few nicks and cuts later, we were finished.

"Look at how good you look, papi. I got me a motherfuckin' man in my house! Don't worry, baby, the blood will stop. Just put this tissue on your face."

If I had known when something was truly sexy, I would have been on extra-horny status. But it was a good thing that this little interlude wasn't an arousing one, because that type of feeling would have belittled the entire experience. *The Graduate in the Hood* was not happening that afternoon. Here was a woman, not even a relative, who took time out of her day to help a little knucklehead discover some man shit. That was DLM #3. Even though I feel that fathers should be around to show, and explain, the ropes of masculinity, I'm sure that many men are forced to discover their masculine aspects through encounters with the women in their lives. This is one reason why, in my most humble opinion, no one can agree on what being a man is. There are so many female influences that it is rather difficult to separate those from the male ones. Especially if you have only females in your life.

Surprisingly enough, a woman also revealed to me how to deliver high-quality ass whoopings. My auntie taught me how to fight. Well, she didn't teach me how to fight, exactly; it was more how-to-pick-shit-up-and-hit-a-motherfucker-in-the-head training.

My auntie was an urban warfare specialist. She was the Q to my James Bond, outfitting me with unconventional weapons and instructing me in their uses. The first gadget she ever issued to me was a sock filled with change that had a zipper to close it up.

"Why does it have a zipper on it, Auntie? Why didn't you just tie a knot in it?" I ignorantly asked.

"A knot makes it shorter and you have to get closer to that motherfucker to hit his ass. With a zipper, after you done smashed him in his teeth, you can jump on a bus, zip open the sock, pay the fare, and get away." After a little thought, her explanation made perfect sense.

The next weapon that I received could have caused me to catch a felony case, if I were caught with it. My auntie gave me a midsized green water pistol filled with Clorox bleach. She put it in a sandwich bag and handed it over to me with much ceremony.

"This one, baby, is the last resort. If you can't kick that motherfucker in the dick, knock him in the head, or stab him in the throat, take this out and squirt his ass in the eyes a few times. Bet you he'll stop fuckin' with you then, huh?" God bless her. Her instruction saved my life a couple of times.

I once went to the store to pick up some butter and flour for my auntie, and a couple of dope fiends tried to rob me. I saw them following, but I figured that, like most fiends, they'd forget about me after I entered the store. Not these. As soon as I exited, one grabbed my arm and the other tried to snatch the bag of groceries. The whole scene was like the two *Velociraptors* attacking the *T. rex* in *Jurassic Park*. I was struggling, they were all over me, and all of us were making an unholy racket. The bag fell, and the food spilled all over the place. The fiends immediately hit the ground and tried to stuff their pockets with my auntie's groceries. I reached into the pocket of my bootleg Members Only jacket and retrieved the quarter-stuffed sock. I started whaling on the crackheads. They were tough, shrugging off my first couple of blows. Then I hit one in the cheek, and all of us heard a loud crack! Dude's face was indented. His hand shot up to his newly deformed cheek, and he started crying. His partner flinched, as if he were about to rush me. I raised the sock over my head, and he changed his mind. After cussing me out and making unenforceable threats, they oozed away. As I returned the groceries to the bag, I silently thanked my auntie, over and over.

I guess I was lucky to have people like my auntie in my life, but like a lot of boys in my situation, I wanted my pops. I wanted to play catch with him, maybe go to the barbershop and kick it with him and his friends. But it was not going to happen. I was on my own.

I was ten years old when I joined my first support group. It was called, I shit you not, the Sperm Donors Club.

One of my older friends, Brad, was bitter about his father being MIA. He was always pissed and would snap at a moment's notice. One day we were all kickin' it in front of the bodega when this old lady bumped into Brad, knocking him out of her way. She looked at him all disgusted.

"Why are you out here doing nothing? Where is your father?"

"You mean my sperm donor? Your guess is as good as mine, you old bitch," he said with more venom than I'd ever heard.

Sperm donor—a perfect synonym for the fathers in my neighborhood. And that was the day that the Sperm Donors Club was formed. We would gather like ravens on the tallest playground structure in the courtyard of our projects, telling each other made-up stories about our imaginary fathers. Mario Gonzales always had the best and the shortest stories.

"All right, see—me and my papi was riding on these superfast bikes, right? And we were going so fast that the cops tried to pull us over—and—and my papi grabbed the cop's gun and hit the cop in the head with it. The cop crashed and couldn't chase us no more, so we went home and had my mom fry up some platanos. Yep, just like that."

Every time we told these stories, we mythologized our fathers. We turned them into these incredible heroes who could do no wrong and who performed amazing feats of strength, shit that we knew nobody could ever do. Somehow it helped to ease the pain, if only a little.

Most of my crew from the Sperm Donors Club have children now. It's a trip to think about angry Brad and silly-ass Mario and all the rest of those cats as fathers now. As I'm writing this, my wife is eight weeks pregnant, and I cannot tell you how freaked I am. I want nothing more than to be a good father, and I hope that I don't screw up my future son or daughter. The old Donors crew and me are not as tight as we used to be, but I caught up with a couple of them.

Brad has two kids, works for juvenile detention, and has been married for over fourteen years. From what my people back home say, he's a great father but not the best husband. He seems to have a bit of a wandering dick. I asked him if he remembered our talks—our lies—about our fathers. He laughed and said that it was those talks that helped him stick around for his daughters. And before I asked, he told me about his philandering. There was no guilt in his admission, just his side of the story. He told me that he and his wife are more like roommates than lovers. Apparently they went to counseling, his suggestion, but she wasn't really feeling it. She tells him that she still loves him, but after fourteen years of marriage, she was stuck as to how to keep the relationship moving. Broke my heart. I playfully warned him that he'd better be good to those girls, or I'd beat his ass. He laughed and promised me that he wouldn't become another sperm donor.

On a more depressing note, Mario died in 2006. He left a girlfriend and a daughter behind. Another father gone.

Some people say that the worst part of growing up in a single-parent household is that you don't get equal male and female influences. It's said that boys of single mothers turn out to be sissies and pampered, that girls raised solely by their fathers become these near-pedophilic treasures, fetish objects of their daddys. While some of this may be true, the single worst thing, for me, was growing up broke as hell. Seeing all of the other kids with GI Joe and skateboards and nice clothes hurt. What did these kids do to have such nice stuff? Why didn't my mom make enough money so that I could have nice things? Shameful as it is to admit, it was my mother's lack of showering me with material objects that caused me to dislike her.

It was as if she didn't love me. Buying and making me wear hand-me-downs, no-name shoes, and corduroy pants and vest sets was cruel. I was a smart kid, and instead of going to the poorly achieving school in my neighborhood, I was sent off to a school where intelligence, even for black folks, was applauded. Translation: I was an experiment. Could a black dude academically achieve? We called it the handout program. I went to a predominantly white school where most of the kids came from affluent families. So while the majority of my schoolmates were wearing the latest and greatest, I looked like a Sears mannequin—from sixteen years ago. I took my mother's poverty as a personal affront. My kid logic interpreted the situation as she was being broke on purpose, like she was hiding from money just so she could ruin my social life.

About two years ago, she and I actually spoke about our past. Every other time that I had tried to bring something up, she'd deftly switch the subject. And not wanting to fight her, I'd ride the segue train. But on that particular day, I held my ground. I questioned her as to why we were so broke. And without missing a beat, she told me that I was an accident and that it took her damn near fifteen years to adjust to the fact that she had a kid.

Damn. Talk about a blow to the heart. We haven't spoken about our past since.

Welfare Willie, Free-Lunch Freddie

Being broke in your own neighborhood was no big deal because everyone else was broke. But being broke at school was an entirely different matter. Other kids came in wearing their Swatches and their Benetton or Coca-Cola rugby shirts, but there I was, in a powder blue T-shirt, one size too small, with a faded Shaun Cassidy decal on the front.

And I'm a dude.

That shit does not go over well in school because kids are the most evil bastards in the entire world. I'm wearing the Shaun Cassidy T-shirt, brown corduroys, and fake Chuck Taylors that my mom bought from the drugstore, and I'm standing in the free-lunch line. That nuclear fluorescent orange food voucher in my hand, ready to eat what the U.S. government deemed healthy for the children of non-economically viable families: hard bread, thick peanut butter, a handful of raisins, a nugget of yellowish cheese, a soggy-ass bologna sandwich, and a miniature carton of week-old milk.

Buying my lunch was not an option because we were so broke that I had never even had a birthday party. Well, that could be because my grandmother was a Jehovah's Witness, and her influence over my mom was more powerful than I thought. But I still never had a party.

We had no extra money, so it was free lunch until some "extra money" made itself available or something else happened. This something else happened after a particularly intense day of being teased in the lunch line.

"Welfare baby. We need somebody to clean our house—ask your mom if she wants a job."

The insults were bad, but when those little fuckers started to make up songs, that was just too much.

"Welfare Willie, Free-Lunch Freddie, you eat bologna when we eat spaghetti!"

Most of my fellow free-lunchers seemed to be immune to the taunts, but I had had enough. It was such a simple thing to do.

A chrome banister separated the free-lunch and the regular-lunch lines. On the other side, in the Promised Land, were little tables where the good food was. Those little tinfoil containers gleamed like a treasure of silver coins.

I followed the familiar path to collect my anti-nourishment, but instead of going to the end of the line, I drifted over to the chrome barrier. I glanced around a couple of times, making sure that no one was looking at me. Then I shot my hand over to the forbidden zone, and it came back with a burrito. I covered it with a napkin, completed the circuit of humiliation, presented my food voucher to the lunch lady—who looked at me like I was contagious—collected my soggy brown bag, and took a seat at the far end of the lunchroom.

I gathered all of my homies around and unveiled my prize like I was a magician: *voila!* Silence. I took out the dirty spork that was issued with the free lunch, and I ripped the burrito into little sections and gave them to my friends. We all looked at each other and we knew that if we ate this ill-gotten piece of food, we could never go back to free lunch. I felt like I was a dope pusher: "Here you go, man. Nah, don't even worry about that. The first one is free. Get me back next time."

While everyone stared down at their little chunk of burrito, mesmerized by the steam rising from it, Jeffy, this enormous kid who spoke maybe three words a week, said, "We ain't got no taco sauce."

And then he was off like a golem whose only purpose was to get some taco sauce. He stalked to the food stations and came back almost immediately, too fast for him to have retrieved anything. Jeffy dug his hands into his pockets, and when he pulled them out again, it was as if a piñata had exploded; we were showered with dozens of little foil taco sauce packets. "Let's eat, y'all." And we all reverently ate the food as if it were holy.

Two things happened that afternoon. First, Jeffy and I became boys. I had found a connection to another male, something that I had been searching for longer than I could remember. A connection that didn't involve sports or violence or anything else that could cause grievous bodily harm. If I couldn't have a father, at least I could have a best friend, right? The second thing was that I discovered the absolute joy of stealing.

When I found out that I had an almost supernatural talent for theft, it was like I had just been bitten by a radioactive spider or bombarded by gamma rays or come from another planet with powers far beyond those of mortal men. I had found my calling; my true nature was revealed: Shawn Taylor, professional thief. And my boy, Jeffy, became my loyal apprentice.

Getting the good lunch started becoming way too easy. A burrito one day, that little rectangular pizza slab the next day, the compressed, breaded turkey drummie ball on a stick the day after that. *The prince of ghetto thieves was supremely bored.* I needed further amusement.

Sixth months after he and I made this cosmic connection, Jeffy moved away. His mom was seeing this really nice dude who got a job down in Atlanta. He took them with him. But before Jeffy left, I tried to coerce him into one more job.

Upon reflection, being an eighth-grader and trying to mastermind a major criminal action seems a little incongruous. I was supposed to be worrying about action figures and playing sports, not petty theft. But poverty has a way of making you do things that you shouldn't. Plus, stealing was so fun.

"Hey, Jeffy. Since you're leaving on Saturday, we got to do something big. So you won't forget where you come from."

"How big is big?"

"A car," I said, cracking a tiny smile.

"You crazy, dude. I cain't be doin' that."

"Look, I've been doin' this shit for a little while. It ain't hard. We just drive around a minute, and when we're done, we bring it down to Ramon's, and he gives us some money for it. It's easy. Look, I'll get the car; you just be lookout."

We went over to the park because that's where the nicer cars were.

"All right, man. Keep your eyes open," I ordered him, slipping into sneak-thief mode.

I broke out my tools and started to work. Jeffy got nervous.

"I don't know, man. We going down south in a few days; we gonna have some money. I don't even be needing to do this no more. Look at these sneakers. I didn't even have to boost 'em. My new daddy just walked into the store and bought them." His words pissed me off.

"I ain't got me a new daddy to buy me shit. I need this money."

"We get to start over," Jeffy pleaded. "I ain't about to mess this up. You doin' this out of fun, not because you need something. How about I ask my momma if you can come with us?"

DLM #4: a male offering something to me because he cared, not because he wanted something in return.

"I need this." I tried to convince both of us.

"I got to go."

Jeffy, my best friend, my boosting buddy, walked out of my life and into his future. I didn't feel like boosting the car after he left, so I picked up my tools and bounced home with an enormous lump in my throat. I wanted to cry so badly. My best friend in life was about to leave me, but real men didn't cry. That's what the "real men" in my neighborhood told me.

Imagine that a skinny, snaggle-toothed weed smoker is saying the following:

> (Inhale) Youngblood, it's like this—you don't never let nobody see you cry. Because if you do, they will think that you're a pussy and they'll fuck with you until you die. (Exhale) If you must cry, I mean you can't (inhale) punch a dude in the face, and you have to cry, do it in front of a woman. You'll get some pussy for sure then. Bitches love that sensitive shit. (Exhale)

And with that oh-so-intelligent advice, my emotional capacity was ruined all to hell.

If you really want to see a man try to crawl out of his skin, watch him around someone who is crying. I'll tell you, it still freaks me the fuck out. My wife is very free with her tears. They're kind of like a baptism for her, a cleansing type of thing. I can't take it 'cause I have no idea what to do. Do I let her cry on my shoulder with all of the spit and snot and emotions, or do I get her a Kleenex and change the subject?

All of this real-men-don't-cry shit has retarded my feelings. Well, not exactly my feelings, but how I show and process them. Try as I might, I cannot muster any empathy for someone who is crying. If someone is pissed off, angry, I can understand that—"I feel your pain, dude." If they're in tears, I'll always make a joke, like an idiot, so they'll stop it.

"Hey, who do you think would win in a fight—them cats from *Miami Vice* or Starsky and Hutch?" People will usually laugh just to get me to shut up and let them have their tears and sadness.

Emotion
Commotion

One of the first and only times in my youth that I cried from something other than physical pain was when Mr. Spock died in *Star Trek II*. He was behind that glass, and Dr. McCoy was just looking at him, all helpless and whatnot. Then they had this conversation, and I felt my eyes get all misty. Then Spock died, and I was like, "Why God, why? Spock was my main man!" And the waterworks began.

It wouldn't have been that big of a deal, except for the fact that I was with my biggest, baddest, most thugged-out friends. Why big, bad thugs were watching *Star Trek* I have no idea.

The projects were like prison when it came to tears—show any type of weakness and you were fucked. Where I grew up, tears were the ultimate sign of weakness; they were an ass-whooping magnet. Here I was, crying over some fictional character, not even thinking that at that very moment every dude in the room was sizing me up and restructuring what they thought about me.

On the one hand, they saw me do my dirt and knew that I was just as wild as they were. On the other hand, I did my homework on time and read books for fun, so I was between a five and an eight on the *Pussy Index* (P.I.). The Pussy Index was a scale of how much of a pussy you were. Every activity had a number associated with it. If you stole something, you had a P.I. of zero. If you stole something and it was makeup for a girl that you liked, your P.I. could hover around ten or eleven.

The numbers of the P.I. were like karma—you couldn't do a thing about them unless you did something to negate the score that you had received. Say that a couple of weeks back you sneaked a peek at your homeboy's dick while you were at the piss trough at school and got a score of around fifty. You would have to do something unapologetically male (stupid) to counteract that transgression. Some drastic shit was needed before you wound up with no friends (or enemies), just a bunch of boys confused about their own sexuality treating you like a pariah. This drastic shit usually revolved around the possibility that you might die or become crippled or disfigured.

There was this one dude who tried to dissolve a particularly high P.I. rating by jumping from his balcony to a tree. He missed the branch that he was aiming for, and his face kissed every part of the tree on his way down. For the rest of that year, his face looked like it was hit by a hot bag of nickels, but he had a negative P.I. rating for the rest of his life. That kid was he-man emeritus. He could've started wearing high heels, no shirt, a bow tie, and leopard-skin drawers, and all we would've said was, "He on a different level. He can do whatever he wants to. He fell through a tree, hit the ground, was still alive, woke up, and walked back up to his house. No pussy would've survived that shit, right?"

I'm about to sound like a brainwashed soldier here, but I didn't make up the rules. I just followed them. Back to *Star Trek*.

OK, so the credits were rolling, and all these cats are just staring at me. Cameron brushed by me to eject the tape, but as he bent down to the VCR, he shot his leg out and kicked my chair out from under me. I hit the ground, and the entire living room fell out laughing. I had never seen a bunch of kids laugh so goddamn hard in my life.

Something came over me, something that I never felt before—rage! Oh, what a glorious feeling! Let me explain something to you: Rage is not an emotion. Rage is an old man who lives in the pit of your stomach and has just four words of advice for you: "Kick all they asses!"

I scanned the room to see who would be the easiest to take out. Why not take out the cat who embarrassed me first and then just work my way around the room? Sounded like a plan to me. I jumped up from the ground, grabbed Cameron by his ears, and then bit him right on his forehead. I leapt from him and tried to take everyone out, lost in a ghetto berserker fit. When I calmed down and regained my senses, I was underneath six cats who were all apologizing to me.

"Yo, B, we was just fucking around with you. You be snappin' all the time. Are you cool now?" I gave them the don't-ever-let-this-shit-happen-again look, and they all got off me, a little scared. P.I. rating of zero.

Seeing these tough guys look at me with a little fear in their eyes made me feel really good, safe. I was safe in the knowledge that these people, who claimed to be my friends, were going to think twice about ever putting their hands on me again.

Where I came from, being known as a crazy, violent motherfucker was better protection than a bulletproof vest. Now, what kind of silly shit is that? Being safe because people are afraid of you and your capacity for violence?

Violence
Is Easy

Violence, as sick as it is, is one of the only acceptable ways for men to express themselves in Western society. We are expected to settle disputes with our fists. This is because throughout "man history" we've been beating the crap out of everything we came into contact with.

This has been going on for God, Allah, Jah, Buddha, Vishnu knows how long.

Everyone has an aggressive side, a violent side, but ours (men) seems to be just a little closer to the surface than that of our female counterparts. For some reason, we feel as if we don't have the time or tools to dig the tunnel or climb the mountain; we just get some dynamite and blast a big, jagged hole right through it. It's easier.

Folks say that violence is a learned behavior. I don't believe that for a minute. Boxing, karate, and escrima are learned; violence is as natural as the ass crack. If people paid more attention to their boy children, just as the violent programming starts to kick in, and didn't write off their aggressive behavior as "boys will be boys," they could help get these impulses under control. There is nothing wrong with aggressive impulses. It is the way that we process and act on them that causes untold amounts of hurt.

Maybe parents could actually spend some time with their children and find alternatives to their aggressive and violent tendencies. The problem arises when this behavior goes unchecked. The little boys really start to dig violence and grow into men who really dig violence. Let's get real, the fist is mightier than talking and listening.

The most addictive thing on this planet is not sex, drugs, alcohol, or even television. The most addictive thing on this planet is an act of physical violence. More specifically, an act of physical violence that will not be retaliated against. When you know that you can put your hands on somebody, hurt and humiliate him, and not have to worry about losing the fight or watching your back, there isn't another feeling like it.

When I discovered the power that was in my fist, it was like King Arthur pulling Excalibur from the stone. I knew that by using my fist nothing could stop me. I would be the king of my world.

My initiation into the true power of the fist came at a time in my life when I was powerless. I was a very bright kid, but I was also a broke-ass project rat, and my uppity classmates, as always, would remind me of this every chance that they got.

Back in the day, I was the only brother into Dungeons and Dragons and fantasy novels and science fiction, so, out of self-preservation, I kicked it with the audiovisual, chess club–type kids at school. But back on the block, I had to code-switch and hang out with the thugs and thieves, because I couldn't exactly explain a "plus two sword" to my hood friends. My D&D buddies taunted me to no end, but I still hung in there, enduring it all. These (mostly white) folks were kind of like my passport out of my (mostly black and despairing) existence. It's probably the same reason that many black professional athletes date white women. They want to leave their old world behind and enter a new one where (hopefully) their past and their skin color are points of interest or curiosities and not detriments.

So I was a crazy hoodlum in the projects, but I was an Oreo (you know, black on the outside but white on the inside) at school. A young man cannot keep up this warped double-consciousness thing for long. Something has to give, and the thing that usually gives is self-control. That's what happened to me.

My AP English class was going to go on a field trip, and, as usual, I didn't have the money to go. I was asking the teacher about scholarships when this little *Village of the Damned*–looking white boy says to me, "Gosh, Shawn, don't you ever have any money?"

I saw nothing but red and heard nothing but the heavy breathing of the ghetto.

I was a black Bruce Banner, about to turn into an Afroed Incredible Hulk. "Don't make me black. You wouldn't like me when I'm black."

A crowd of these bastards formed around the teacher's desk and started laughing and pointing until my right fist started to twitch and I had an epiphany—I knew, right then, that if I used my fist on one of their faces, the laughter would stop. They wouldn't tease me anymore. I knew that all I had to do was cock my fist back, just like an arrow, and let it fly; I'd have no more problems. And I did just that. Blam! All the teacher did, probably could do, was watch. He watched the kids go at me, and he watched as I beat some ass.

It was as if my fist had a mind of its own. From my side to that kid's nose, in the blink of an eye. The moment when my hand met his face it felt so damn good. For once I had some power, enough power to not let anyone hurt me. I looked down at him.

"Now what, motherfucker? Kind of hard to talk shit when you're choking on your blood and teeth, ain't it? Where are your fucking jokes now, bitch?"

The teacher looked as if he were about to have a heart attack. I really thought about giving him one to the jaw, but he was kind of big, and I didn't think I could take him. But I wanted to hit him so badly for not intervening when my classmates were teasing me.

All of the kids—and the teacher—backed up and looked at me differently. They knew that I was the last guy in the world that they should be fucking around with.

I may have gotten suspended (wasn't the first or the last time), but when I got back to school, I was a member of the elite. Not the monetary elite, but the only elite class that truly matters: I was now one of the tough kids. I was dangerous! I was a bad boy! No more kicking it with nerd groups. I was on a different level.

Any man who has ever been the bad boy can tell you that there is nothing like it. You were handy with your fists, quick at the mouth, and every other boy—whether they admitted it or not—secretly wanted to be you, while the girls wanted to get with you. After you have been the bad boy for a while, you no longer even have to do much bad shit to keep the title. Your reputation will take care of that for you.

Don't get me wrong, you still had to knock somebody out or tell a teacher to shut the fuck up, but your rep was your ticket. Keep in mind, though, that your rep had to be tended like a garden, trimming the weeds and watering it every so often so that it would flourish and grow the way that you wanted. Most of the time you never had to present your rep, because the school kids would do it for you. They'd pump it up through the stratosphere! And like the misguided little man-children that we were, we reveled in it.

We agreed with every single lie and exaggeration, mythologizing ourselves like some of us did our fathers. We were these small, scared-to-death boys living inside these larger-than-life costumes.

A few of us have carried that adolescent bad-boy shit with us as we have gotten older, and we really, truly, believe our legends; we move through our lives as caricatures.

"I'm tough, man! You better watch out! I'm such a bad motherfucker that I can bench-press God!"

It's like Arnold Schwarzenegger believing that he is really jumping out of airplanes and fighting terrorists, while the stupid-ass audience believes it too. It's that bad. This whole rep thing causes men to have split personalities.

Have you ever met one of those guys who, one-on-one, is the coolest sonuvabitch in the entire world, but when he has an audience he has to perform—live up to his reputation? And after witnessing his behavioral flip-flop on several different occasions, you want to beat him with a flaming baseball bat? That was what I had become.

My business card was my fists and feet. I must have been in a couple hundred street fights. I won some, I lost some, but I never backed down. Fighting was my life raft. If I didn't have it, what did I have? My intellect wasn't valid in any of my social circles, but you couldn't dismiss my ability to beat the ever-loving shit out of someone. After a while, my violent acts were no longer tools for empowerment; the shit became habitual. There were two major events that helped me break my addiction to violence.

I met this dude named Andrew Kuroiwa, who was a junior judo instructor. He was a schoolmate who'd seen me scrap a few times at school and approached me about my motivations—pointing out that I never threw the first punch but would taunt my opponents enough so they'd attack me; then I could feel justified about beating them down. Andrew was damned perceptive. He told me about how he used to be the same way but found an outlet through sport judo. He gave me a couple of lessons, and I competed in a couple of matches. I didn't do too well, but I found a release valve for my violence. When I felt the urge to fight—if it wasn't a self-defense situation—I'd go to the gym and spar. Just as I found this bit of near peace, Tad was shot.

Tad was like me, a closet Afro-geek. We read and traded comic books, but we also had each other's backs in the streets. If I fought, he fought, and vice versa. Between our sophomore and junior years, Tad started to sell weed. A nickel here, a dime there—not much looking in from the outside but enough to get noticed and known. He had a truck, nice clothes, chains, and an addiction to his new lifestyle.

One day we skipped school and decided to eat at White Castle. We were walking out with two big bags of burgers when a car skidded around the corner, and I heard an unholy cough. Tad spun around and slammed, in a heap, on the sidewalk. The car peeled off, and Tad was wiggling, mewling, and crying on the ground. I turned him over, and his left cheek was missing. Blood and flesh were everywhere. His teeth were streaked with pencil-thin ropes of fleshy redness. Someone called an ambulance and Tad was taken to the hospital. Even though he made it, he was permanently disfigured. My boy had become a monster. I could barely look him in his face. After a while, my discomfort with his new look created an irreparable tear in our relationship, and I abandoned him. Taking Tad's facial disfigurement as a cue, I made an effort to not engage in unnecessary violence. If someone came at me, I'd give it to them, but I was no longer going to seek out physical conflict. The cost was way too high for continuing a violent lifestyle. But without the pressure release that comes with the commission of violent acts, I began holding in my emotions. And by doing this, it corrupted my interpersonal relationships, especially when it came to intimacy.

Emotion Commotion II

When I was younger, I could be intimate with a single person, but the only way that I could feel connected within a group was to either loudly talk shit or throw punches. I craved nonsexual physical contact from men but had no idea how to ask for it appropriately. I know I am not alone in this either. One day, take a look at how men hug. We can't just hug; we have to pound the shit out of each other's backs.

"What's up, dog?" Brothers intricately shake hands, then they pull each other close—making sure that their arms form a hetero-barrier between them—and then clasp for no more than four seconds. Hard! Pow! Somewhere in our minds we think that four seconds is just enough time before we enter gay territory. After the hug, we check our surroundings to make sure that what people saw was just a friendly hug and not a precursor to some later homosexual act. We might even throw a punch to the shoulder, just to assert our masculinity. We do this to show that we aren't homos.

When I was growing up, it was as if some covert machine was implanting subliminal hate messages directly into my brain. For all of my life, I have been told about the horrors of homosexuality: ass fucking, dick sucking, and tossing salads. Things that you should do only with or to females. If you were doing this stuff to anyone who was not a woman, you were the lowest of the low and deserved to get the shit beat out of you. Because of this, I was homophobic for as long as I could remember. Well, not exactly homophobic, more like homo-hatred: a complete, total, and utter hatred and disgust for homosexuals. But I have evolved. I am now neither homophobic nor homo-hating. I am homo-uneasy. Queer folk still make me feel kind of uncomfortable, but I'm working on it. Admittedly, I have a very long way to go before I reach homo-clear.

Maybe this comes from being a black male. Out of all of my "United Colors of Benetton"–looking friends, the black men are the least tolerant of queerdom. I'm sure you've heard the various explanations as to why brothers are so homophobic. Let me paraphrase a common theory: Throughout history, slavery, colonialism, Christian dominance, and whatnot, black men have been emasculated and their sexuality turned into a poison. The very thought of being treated, in any way, as a female or being put into a sexually subservient position is the ultimate insult. Having had our manhood shaped and reshaped dozens of times over, we can't even stand the thought of not being able to be a "full man."

That's one theory, and it makes sense. It isn't right (as in right or wrong), but it makes sense. Guess what, though? I have my own theory.

One of the main reasons, in my humble opinion, that my folks don't dig on the gay thing is that black male existence exists in a paradoxical state in relation to homosexuality. Almost all of our popular social culture, from dancing to sports, is highly homoerotic. LL Cool J is not just licking his lips for the ladies. Football players hug and wrestle and smack one another on the asses. When I was coming up, every young brother wanted to be Billy Dee Williams. And when many of us discovered Prince and Rick James, we were so confused. We didn't know whether we wanted to be those cats or were attracted to them. Black male social life is wrought with homo-eroticism, but we have been inundated with antihomosexual propaganda so we don't "turn gay." You cannot be black and gay. It just isn't allowed. So we overreact to anything even remotely resembling homosexuality. It's kind of like black police officers being twice as hard on black perps. You see a little bit of yourself in the other, and you hate them and your-self for that other person's actions.

I do not believe for a minute that every man—deep down inside—has a gay person raging to get out. That's bullshit. What I'm talking about is the wanting of a male relationship that is more multidimensional than the ones we currently have. Aside from a very few select cases, most of my interac-tions with men orbit around music, women, or (God forbid) cars. I could just imagine the looks on my boys' faces if I broke out one day and said, "Yo, man! Have you ever woken up in the middle of the night, all agitated, sweaty, and shivering? You put some clothes on, go outside, sit down on some grass, and look up at that big beautiful moon. You're sitting there, just chillin' in nature, listening to the animals rustle the grass, the owl hooting, and the breeze running through the trees. Then you begin to think to yourself, with all of this around me—this nature, this beauty—why do I feel so disconnected from it all?"

Nobody would say shit for a little while and then, "What's with this sensitive vibe, man? You on some P.M. Dawn–type mess right here. I ain't with that gay shit."

I would be clowned to no end. And that's a goddamn shame!

I don't know about other men, but I crave something more meaningful than a conversation about whether or not this or that girl's titties are real. I want to talk about death and religion and dreams. Hell, I might even want to talk about the type of couch I want to buy. *I'm straight, but I want to decorate!* What's wrong with that? Have our egos and self-images been so corrupted that we can't live our lives without questioning our own (or our friends') sexuality in the process?

"Damn, dude. What the fuck you buy that light blue sweater for? You getting a little bit soft around here."

Soft and hard. Hard is desirable, while anything soft is to be shunned. Hard is masculine, and soft is feminine. It's kind of easy to figure out how that came to be, but most of our perceptions as to what is soft or hard taint our worldviews.

"He's a stone-cold killer." Stones are hard, and this is said with reverence.

"That cat's so wishy-washy." *Wishy-washy* is said with disgust. It even sounds soft, doesn't it?

Now, check this out—this is where all of the hard and soft shit gets twisted: music! There is nothing that will have men question your sexuality more than the music that you listen to. I wouldn't even dare to show some of my boys my entire music collection. If I did, I would have to field millions of questions.

"Yo, what the fuck is a B-Jork?"

"Now, who is this white chick? Tor-I Amos? Is this some Amos 'n' Andy shit?"

"Her name is Tori Amos," I would plead, "and she sings . . . rock. 'God, sometimes you don't come through. Do you need a woman to look after you?'"

"You better stop clownin' before your ass gets struck down up in here. You getting soft on me, or what? With all of this shit, you're gonna start making a brother wonder about you. And one thing I know is that I better not see no *Rent* soundtrack or some Barbara Streisand shit up in here. This I know." Come to think of it, I do have the *Rent* soundtrack.

Let's follow this musical thread a bit further. How my male friends think of soft and hard really trips me out. Any of these new ignorant, young boy rappers who talk about killing people or have a bunch of half-naked women in their videos, dousing them with liquor or claiming that "we don't love these hoes"—most of my friends consider them hard. They are to be emulated and their footsteps closely followed.

Now just mention somebody like Ben Harper or Lenny Kravitz, who had a song titled "Let Love Rule."

Let love rule, not pour champagne on it and call it a bitch. Let it rule over us, our lives, the world. Love. I'm not the biggest Lenny Kravitz fan, but I want to illustrate a point. Just mention this to most of my boys, and this is what you will get in return:

"That's gay shit, man. What hard nigga is gonna be talking about letting somebody's love rule? That's soft; bitch, shit. You see how that cat dresses? Just look at his ass and you can just tell that he's as gay as Sylvester and Tevin Campbell at Liberace's house."

"You know that he was with Lisa Bonet, right?" I'd say.

"Babe from *The Cosby Show*?"

"Yep."

"Yo, she was in that spooky *Angel Heart* shit, though. She don't even count."

That's Gay, Dude

Back in college I had a gay friend, Michael. My boys and I would watch him get ready before going to the club. We were trying to soak up game because women would just orbit him like he was the sun. He would come out of the shower with just a towel wrapped around his ass—he would do this to make us feel uncomfortable—washboard abs gleaming like brushed onyx, and then he would lay out four or five different outfits.

While the rest of us would be trying to pass off black jeans as dress pants, he would really have some dress pants laid out, along with various types of dress shirts and blazers, all kinds of shit, way more fashionable than any of the stuff we had. He would then get his accessories on: Guess? watch, gold ring and necklace, some weird patterned socks, and then one of over what seemed like a million leather or ostrich belts. He would top the whole thing off with some type of shoe or boot that none of us had ever seen before. They had either a buckle or a zipper, or maybe they were slip-ons, but never any laces. I asked him about this once, and he gave me a look that could only be interpreted as "They're Italian, peasant."

Watching him with all of his gear led me to believe that there was a slush fund for young gay males into which they could dip and get money to buy their clothes. We were college students, and his parents were broke, so this could be the only explanation.

OK, we would hit the club, and some unique things would happen. First off, he would never get carded or charged. Our fake IDs would be scrutinized to no end, but he would waltz on through the doors as if he owned the place. When we were all finally allowed to enter, we would catch up to Michael, and he would be standing at the edge of the dance floor, every single eye on him. Dudes were sizing him up and pulling their women closer, and the women were conjuring every single sexual fantasy that their imaginations could handle. We wanted some of his shine, so like a demented version of Fat Albert and the Cosby kids, we'd rush up behind him. "This is our friend. He's with us."

He'd put one foot on the dance floor like an Africanized John Travolta, hips swaying to the music. His other foot would join the first and people would start to back up, and then he would turn the beat around and dance his ass off.

See, real men didn't dance (unless it was b-boying), so we were lined up like a murder of crows, nodding our heads to the thump-thumping of the music. All of our dancing was done from the neck up. One by one, women of all colors would get their boogies on with him. He'd freak one and spin her off only to freak another and then another, moving like he was the music.

"See," Tremayne said, "he can't be gay. Look how he's dancing with those chicks." But T spoke too soon. Michael's opposite number stepped onto the dance floor. He was just as well dressed and as handsome. Michael's eyes lit up as they stalked each other like animals on *Mutual of Omaha's Wild Kingdom*. They stood toe-to-toe, and there wasn't anybody in that entire place but them. The misfit crew and I were staring at them, our heads cocked to the side. "Ahhhh!" And Tremayne, with his silly ass, "Yo, that's gay, dude." We all straightened up and put fake-ass disgusted scowls on our faces. "Yeah, that is gay."

"Well, he is gay," I said.

The two men danced until last call. There were looks of relief on the faces of the men and looks of disappointment mixed with looks of "I think I can change him" in the eyes of the women. So we decided that it was our job to console these women who were in sour spirits.

"Hey, I like the way that you were dancing. How about you give me your number and then we can go dancing together?" Still looking over at Michael, the women were all, "Here, just take it. Take it."

"This is your real number, right? Okay, cool. I'ma call you, for real."

A point of trivia: Michael and Steve, his dancing partner from that night, are still together. Fifteen or so years together as a gay black couple. Theirs is one of the most successful relationships that I personally know of. And I'm sorry to say, it still creeps me out a bit. My homophobia was undermined by my envy and admiration but only for a little while. I still have these weird irrational little fits of ignorance in my dealings with gay men, but manufactured masculinity and what I consider to be masculine are conditions that are going to take more than my lifetime to change.

Sex

The Great Misadventure

At the time I really started dating, in college, I was just discovering how damaged I truly was—how much I hated my father for not being there and how confused I was about my place in my race and cultures. I was a mess with a couple of steamer trunks full of insecurities. So I figured that sex would be the answer to all of my problems. And since I was half Jamaican and half Puerto Rican, I was supposed to be oversexed.

In the late 1980s and early '90s the whole Afrocentricity movement was jumping off. No gold or diamonds were worn—only red, black, and green beads, leather African medallions, shells, and things like that. Dashikis, jungle boots, berets, kente cloth, and black gloves adorned the most conscious of black men. I wasn't one of them. I was about as unconscious as a person could be.

All of these back-to-African cats had one personality trait in common: they were supremely confident when it came to dealing with women.

"Greetings, my Nubian queen. May I carry your books for you? Where are you going on this most vainglorious day?

Chemistry? Sista, did you know that the Egyptians were the first chemists? Look, how about you and me get together over a cup of tea, and I'll show you a couple of books that will make you proud to be a Nubian. Word. May I use a piece of your paper to get your number?"

That shit worked!

One day you'd see this sister wearing a university sweat-shirt and jeans, rushing to class, and the next she'd be walking two steps behind her new guru wearing whatever pseudo-African fabrics were in fashion at the time and carrying an armload of dandelions. She'd be blissful as hell, almost skipping with a fanatical glee.

It was college, and I was horny. I wanted to meet a woman so that I wouldn't be horny anymore. Isn't that what college is all about? Like it would be that easy. I stepped to one of those Afro-washed sisters and tried to lay down my game.

"How are you doing today? I have you in Anthro, right? I was wondering . . . would you like to, um, maybe grab a burger or something?"

"A burger? Are you kidding? Oh my God! Don't you know that meat is a plot by the white man to keep us fat and listless so that he can keep us under his heel of oppression?" Oh yeah, I forget to mention, being a vegetarian was part of this new African consciousness.

I was hoping to get laid, not listen to public radio, so I apologized and walked away, but much to my surprise, she tapped me on the shoulder.

"Look, brother, let's go get a salad, and we'll build on some things."

One salad became two and then three and then a couple of tea dates, and this led to our first kiss. Textbook romance setting: us, by a lake, with a full moon in the sky. We kissed, kissed again, and all was good until we went back to her pad. She had hieroglyphics and all types of fabrics on her walls.

Photos of Malcolm X and Winnie Mandela in the living room and a set of those big-ass wooden spoons and forks hanging in the kitchen. We stepped through some red, yellow, and green beads into her bedroom, and she lays down on her futon. "I want to give my yoni to you."

"Your what?"

"My yoni, my female energy. My womanhood." She then takes her dress off, and I'm face-to-face with a real, live naked girl.

"Come here, my king."

Every single desire to have sex went right out the window. Terror washed over me, and I started to sweat and shake. In that instant I knew I wasn't ready. It was a brave admission to myself, but it destroyed her ego.

"I'm sorry, I can't do this. I'd be doing it for something other than how I actually feel for you." Full, honest disclosure. You'd figure that this was the right thing to do. No.

"I am offering you the most sweetest of gifts, and you turn it down? What kind of a man are you?"

"I don't know, and that's why I can't be with you or your yoni."

"Just leave." She must have called every single person on campus, because by the time I got back to the housing units, I was greeted with, "Brother, what is wrong with you? You turned down the sweet nectar?"

"Are you a faggot?"

My decision to forgo the yoni may have put me out with my Nubian brothers, but the women were intrigued. So I became a project. Who can get Shawn to fuck her first?

Girls were taking me out to dinner, bringing me to concerts and plays. It was a trip. And then it happened. Just like that. I can't reveal her name, but she was one of those bohemian "whatever, who cares, let's do it" personalities. She was a 180-degree turn from the enlightened sisters on campus.

There was nothing romantic about the event whatsoever. We were watching *Taxi Driver* (with the sound off and listening to the Cure), she got butt naked, I got butt naked, the condom went on, and POW. I was in! For about a minute and a half! When I exploded, it must have sounded like people moving a piano.

We both fell asleep, and I woke up in what I thought was love. Too bad that I was only on her agenda for that night and that night only. I tried to call her, I sent her letters, I even stopped by her pad, but it wasn't happening. There is nothing worse than seeing a dude who's depressed over a girl. Walking zombie-slow, hair uncombed, shower an afterthought—I was pathetic. My feelings were hurt, I was in pain, and I didn't even know what I had done to deserve this torment.

And then one day, I saw her. She gets props for not turning away when she saw me.

"Why did you do this to me? What did I ever do to you? Can I please have another chance?" My voice sounded like a scratched Sade album.

She got straight to the point.

"We had sex, it wasn't that good, and you have way too many other things on your mind. I wouldn't get the attention that I need or deserve."

"What do you mean I have other things on my mind? How would you know? I don't have anything on my mind."

"I had to make the first move. You're nice, but that's about it."

She was gone, and my self-esteem went with her. Once again, my business got around campus, and I was clowned to no end. I figured that I just wasn't cut out to deal with women in any capacity besides friendship. But friendship cut off any possibilities of having sex, and I couldn't have that.

Maybe I would not attempt relationships, feelings, and caring but instead jump straight to the sex and I-have-to-leave part. This led to my let-me-try-to-fuck-everything-in-sight-so-that-I-can-prove-that-I-am-a-man phase. I would stop being humble—well, terrified—and go the opposite direction. I would be the model for black male sexual confidence. And if I had to put up a front to do so, so be it. Don't ask me why I thought this would be a good thing to do, or why I thought it would get me in good with females, because I don't have an answer.

So many of us men who have been dumped believe that we can rebuild the walls of our masculine castle by having as much indiscriminate sex as possible. I guess we feel that since we were so emasculated, the only way to reclaim that lost masculinity is by plumbing the depths of the feminine, spelunking for that (imagined) banished part of us, in hopes of becoming whole. Well, if not whole, then at least we'd have a bunch of freaky sex stories to tell our friends.

That phase was ridiculously pointless. All I accomplished was, well, not really having any sex and leaving a lot of hurt feelings in my wake. After college I had a couple of relationships but didn't have too much sex because sex, which took a lot of broken hearts for me to learn, is powerful. Think about it; if it weren't for sex, there wouldn't be any Internet, DVDs, or people. The Internet wouldn't be what it is if the sex industry hadn't pushed for better technology to better experience the anonymous viewing of sexual acts. DVDs make porn discreet and interactive. And we haven't perfected cloning yet, so we still have to have intercourse. Darn.

Sex is on some *X Files*–type shit, especially if you truly dig the person you are with. Those little electric pulses that run from your partner's fingertips to your skin, your breaths and heartbeats matching rhythm, the sense that both of you have more than two arms each. What I dig the most are the little imperfections in your partner's body—a birthmark, a freckle, a scar. Oh, yeah!

I don't care what people say or do to try to fool themselves into believing that sex is just a physical act. Every time you have sex, you share a sacred moment in time with someone. Damn, that sounded corny, didn't it? But you know I'm right. As far as I'm concerned, lovemaking is one of the only true forms of magic left in this world. This realization is one way that I knew that I was in love with my (now) wife.

When we started seeing each other, we didn't have sex for almost a year, and that was OK. We both understood that if we did have sex, it wasn't going to be some ordinary thing; it was going to be the start of a whole adventure. And we were down for that adventure right on through the whole till-death-do-you-part section of the relationship.

This is a woman who has listened to all of my tales of poverty and violence and petty theft, which are the building blocks of my whole existence, and never once judged me. Not once. Some of the things that I did and have gone through may have shocked her, but she was always there, holding my hand or rubbing my back. When a nightmare woke me up in the middle of the night, she didn't say anything as silly as "It's all going to be OK." But she made sure that she was right there to help me confront the demons.

Don't think that this marriage thing is all gravy, though.

Marriage isn't just a relationship between two people; marriage is also a discipline, kind of like yoga. You have to train yourself so that when you find yourself all pretzel-like, twisted to hell, you will be able to relax and breathe easily.

I'm sure that some people reading this are having problems with my linking sex and marriage. Not for one second do I believe that sex should be reserved for marriage. Some, if not all, of your freakiest, weirdest, *Penthouse Forum*–type sex happens with the people you have no plans to marry. That type of sex is all well and good, but sex is a whole lot better when you are in a committed relationship. Ten, twenty, hell, thirty times better. Trust me, I know.

Hey, if you don't believe me, figure it out for yourself. You may be able to do all of the meta-kinky things you want to do with some jump-off, but then you make sure you get away from her as soon as you can. You can't stand to be in the same room with her after you have fucked, let alone share the same bed. This is how you know that the person you were with was not right for you.

If she was a dime piece before the orgasm and then turned into the sea hag postcoitus, you done made a mistake, my friend. If she stays the dime from the night before and you don't want her to leave your side, you endure the bad breath and the eye crust, then, my friend, you have a winner! And the only way you can even accept this "winner" into your life, the only way that you can even begin to acknowledge her presence, is by making attempts to destroy your ego.

The Ego
Has Landed

Ego: the part of your personality that causes you to say and do stupid shit. Or, how about this: a personality trait that manifests itself in inflated self-importance and the desire to defend this self-importance at all costs.

Most of the men I have met can't be self-confident without reducing someone else to insignificance. Believe it or not, my dear friends, I am among this number. I'm not as bad as I used to be, but that knee-jerk, I'm-the-shit-and-you-are-nothing energy manifests itself, less and less lately, at inopportune times. The ego is good for destroying relationships, especially romantic ones. I think that I have had five serious, committed relationships, and three of those ceased to exist because of the ego virus.

The first of these ended because I thought I could pull off that overly macho shit. When we first began to date, she mentioned how she liked a take-charge type of guy, a guy who could get whatever he wanted through force of will alone. I am the antithesis of macho, but if that was what she wanted, that is exactly what she'd get.

Instead of working with her desire, I hijacked it, magnifying what I thought she wanted and completely changing it. Surprisingly, things were good for a time; however, over a period of months, my macho facade began to crumble, and the truth of my *self* began to leak through.

While the macho mask was falling apart, she exposed me for the poser that I was. When she pointed out the fact that I was indeed being something that I was not, instead of agreeing with her I became cruel. How dare this chick come at me like that? This is what she wanted, wasn't it? I didn't put my hands on her or anything like that, but I took that macho ego vibration to the extreme, and it got ugly. Hell, I was ugly. She called me on my shit, and I just couldn't let it go, nor could I admit that she was right.

I belittled her and attacked her self-esteem every chance I got, thinking, like a fucking idiot, that if I kept being mean, she would have to stick around because she'd have no place else to go. A friend of mine said that I hated myself for not being able to be what my girlfriend wanted me to be, so I made her suffer for my own shortcomings and outright failures. Ouch. She was right; she read the shit as if it were delivered every Sunday. I was a loser, and I had to blame someone, but there was no way I could blame myself. I couldn't be in the wrong—I was the man. It was her fault. It had to be, right? Sick, nasty, disgusting lines of reasoning. More on how I moved through that morass later.

Relationship number two imploded because I seemed to lose the ability to speak in block letters. Every time I spoke with this woman, I spoke in calligraphy. This was when I wanted to be known as an *artist*. An artist couldn't speak in plain language, now could he? An artist had to weave words into a basket of understanding and meaning. Oh yeah, imagine a stream of sentences like the previous one leaping out of my mouth. It was repugnant.

When we create ourselves, most of the information we receive is from outside sources: family, friends, spiritual matters, popular culture, and so forth. We ingest all of this information, and then we filter it, deciding what to keep and what to toss. This process, along with our own inclinations and aptitudes, helps us to form our personalities. Through the wonderful lens of hindsight, I can pinpoint my major influences. But when I was coming up, I wasn't this savvy.

I rejected my direct influences and became a social chameleon. I changed who I was to fit into my surroundings and to stay safe. The less people knew about me, the less I would have to reveal, the safer I'd be. I could bullshit my way through, without letting anyone in. Safety— emotional and physical—was my primary concern. My past was filled with loss and disconnection, and I needed to be anchored to something, someone, so that I could stop feeling so damn alone. And it was so much easier to become than to be.

I felt that I wasn't worth the time or effort to cultivate, and it was so much easier and rewarding to become what others wanted. This way, I didn't have to think, nor did I have to look at myself in the mirror. I no longer had to be the poverty-stricken, broken-home, physically abused little project-dwelling pigeon. I could be anyone. This was about as much freedom as I had ever known.

When I met "Sheila," an entirely new world opened up to me—a world filled with films with little words at the bottom, sushi, barefoot dancing in the rain, poetry readings, and museums. And the people who populated this world weren't nerds. These folks existed on the crossroads of Jimi Hendrix and Tori Amos, motorcycles and walking, *Twin Peaks* and Kurosawa films. And the best part of it was that they were of all different races. In this world I wasn't the only black dude in a crowd of white faces.

But instead of developing and asserting my identity along these lines, I mimicked. And I was good at it too.

One night, on the way back from some foreign film festival, Sheila and I had one of those conversations that forever change your life. One of those conversations that, when it is over, make you feel as if someone had just punched you in the gut in order to force you to open your eyes. This conversation was DLM #5.

It was a perfect night, and I was genuinely happy. We were walking hand in hand when Sheila, as she did quite often, sat down in the middle of the sidewalk. She motioned me to join her, and of course I did. We sat there, cross-legged, staring into each other's eyes, not blinking. She grabbed my hand and sandwiched it between hers and asked, "Who are you, really?"

Now, how in the fuck was I supposed to answer a question like that? *I'm from a planet far, far away . . .*

"I'm not sure I understand what you mean, sweetheart," I replied, testing the waters.

"You're perfect. You know about the film directors that should be known, same with the important writers and musicians. You can tell me what they've written, composed, painted, directed, and you seem to enjoy knowing these things."

"I enjoy them very much, darling," I said, still not sure where she was taking me.

"I'm sure you think you do," she hesitated a bit, "but the more that we share time, I'm beginning to realize that your knowledge of other things is all that I know about you." Was she telling me that I was posing?

"But these things are me," I said, realizing that she was about to expose me for the fraud I was. I added, "my queen," to flatter her.

"Who are you?" she asked forcefully.

"I'm just a humble man—"

"You sound like Steven. Who are you?"

"Just a guy trying to find his way in—"

"Michael says the exact same thing. Who are you?"

Tears were welling up in her eyes. She was really trying to solve the Rubik's Cube of my personality, but she was having the damnedest time doing so. She could try to figure me out all she wanted, but I wasn't going to help. As long as I could keep putting up a front, I would.

We went back and forth like this for a minute: she asking me who I was, me replying, and she pointing out that it was someone else's words I was using. Then she leapt from the top rope, elbow first. "Do you love me?"

"You know you're my light." That had to get to her.

"Shawn, I asked you a direct question. Do you love me?"

"You're the air that I breathe, my star—"

"What is wrong with you? Do you love me?"

"Sheila, what do you think I've been telling you?" I said this with a little bass in my voice, to let her know that I was serious.

"I asked you a simple yes or no question, and you couldn't answer me. You are so filled with everyone else's shit"—I knew then that she was livid because she never swore—"that you couldn't answer a simple yes or no question. All you had to say was yes or no, and you couldn't do that. I hope you figure all your stuff out. You're going to be a great man someday." Sheila had left the building.

So there I was, an emotionally fragile, peasant-shirt-wearing idiot, floating in a pool of his own stupidity, in the middle of a dirty-ass sidewalk. Life has a way of just fucking with you, doesn't it?

And now it is time, my dear comrades, for the hat trick.

This next one is the jewel of the bunch. I sabotaged this relationship with such subtle grace and elegance that I could conduct workshops on the topic. *Today we shall learn how try-*

ing to become a man and make sense of one's world is some-thing that you do before entering a relationship, not during.

I'd just been exposed as an unoriginal, highly confused, unself-aware little boy who had no idea how to be himself. Twice. Being busted out as a fake was getting pretty old, and something had to be done about it. I was so tired of having my flaws tossed in my face, my insecurities paraded around, and my social confusion as a point of discussion. It was time for me to figure out what type of man I wanted to be. How did I want people to think about me? What actions was I going to take to undo the grisly, psychosocial little cage that I had erected around myself?

I had to do something, but I had to find another girlfriend first.

Loneliness is not a good feeling, not good at all, especially when you are about to make attempts at finding your authentic personality. I needed a witness to testify that I was indeed on the correct path. This witness's name was "Terra."

Terra was *at ease*. She was just so damn comfortable. She had a Master's before she was twenty-five, but she wasn't a nerd. No matter the situation, Terra was the focal point. All social compasses pointed to her. I had never wanted anyone more desperately.

This girl shot pool, loved going to the movies (not films, but movies), had a smart mouth and quick wit, plus a devastating right jab for someone so small. Oh, and she was very *comfortable* in the intimate realms of the physical.

We met through some mutual friends and hit it off from jump. The deciding factor in our mutual decision to become a couple happened at a nightclub when some dickhead grabbed her ass, and, without a second thought, she clocked the guy in his jaw, laying him out on the floor. It was like a Tex Avery cartoon—my heart began thumping out of my chest while little hearts burst over my head. This was the woman for me. And I knew she felt the same when she saw me standing next to her with a cue stick in my hands, ready to bash this guy's dome. We were inseparable after that.

Everything was beautiful until I started having something akin to growing pains. I began to transform into one of those people who overanalyze everything about themselves and others because of their inadequacies. Wherever I went, whatever I did, I felt uncomfortable. I didn't fit in with anything or anyone. I kept telling myself that I wasn't good enough. I accepted all of the bad things that happened but rejected anything remotely good or beneficial. Because I didn't deserve anything good, did I?

I wish that I could tell you what brought this on, but all I know is that it sucked because it was such a pathological act. I thought that I was worthless—most likely owing to my failed relationships. And since our relationship was running along smoothly, there had to be something wrong with it. I didn't deserve to be this happy. But I'd be damned if I'd let anyone know that I felt this way about myself.

I was a man, damnit, and I could show no vulnerability.

And thus the dissolution began. I started comparing my current relationship to the previous ones. Why did this girl kiss in public and that one didn't? Why did that one wear thongs and this one only period panties? *She* gave me head, but *she* won't place her mouth anywhere below the belly button. It's enough to make you crazy. The worst part of it is when these questions leave your brain and escape through your lips. I can't imagine anything more devastating to a current partner than being told that she didn't do something that a previous partner did. How fucked up is that?

While attempting to become this authentic masculine entity, I completely forgot there was someone else there. I was so self-involved that Terra was pushed by the wayside as I tried to "figure things out." It must suck being a spectator in this type of situation—looking at someone's life, wanting to help but not being allowed to. You have no idea how to help this person because you've been relegated to observer status.

Every inward thought, every auto-critical thing I did, pushed her farther and farther away. I pretended I was including her in the process, but in truth, she was nothing more than a beautiful, warm body that I needed to have around just so my ego would be satisfied. She became a physical and emotional masturbatory tool, a validation of what I thought my manhood was. I needed to feel as if someone loved me. There is no better ego stroke than that. And it was too bad too, because Terra did love me. I couldn't believe I had sacrificed another woman's feelings on the altar of my ego.

And the most distressing thing was that I felt I was doing her a favor, keeping her locked out of my life. I figured that she could just wait around, and when the final result was ready, she could benefit from all of my hard work. I was a misguided fool. Rule number one: Don't ever compare your relationships. Love never looks or feels the same way. Get the hell out of your own way and enjoy (and appreciate) the ride.

This isn't to say that I have learned my lesson and am now 100 percent self-knowing and that I never hurt anyone's feelings. I'm not saying that at all. I pretty much know what I'm about, and it is a damned good feeling. I'm still discovering new things about myself all the time. Sometimes good, sometimes bad, but every day I am getting a clearer picture of that statue in the stone. And to carry this clichéd, corny idea even further, humility is the world's greatest sculptor.

Being humble is damn near impossible for men of color. We have been told repeatedly that we can't do anything we want and that there will always be barriers to our happiness. Our hyperinflated egos and overconfident swagger help us get through each day without killing ourselves or someone else.

When we are told—overtly or covertly—that we don't measure up to *the* standard, it hurts. But once we discover how to dial down from arrogance to humility, amazing things start happening. This is how I met my wife.

I'm not going to go into too much detail now on how we met, how we didn't get along at first, or how we eventually decided that we were for each other. What I will tell you is that I am now happily married, to a wonderful woman, because I deserve it. Seems like I'm contradicting myself, doesn't it? Be humble, but tell yourself that you are deserving of something? It is not contradictory at all. It is a matter of context.

It is not my goal to come across as some New Agey Berkeley type of emasculated automaton with a feminist agenda. That is not who I am, even though I do identify as a feminist-in-training. It's just that so-called progressive movements and ideologies have co-opted some parts of the English language so much so that I need to make certain explanations clearer.

If I walk into a situation holding my dick, puffing out my chest, and operating on arrogant, entitlement level ten, I may get what I want, but there is a sort of backlash. First, I have to back up this hypermasculine attitude, make sure the facade stays intact for the duration of whatever it is I'm doing. This takes a lot of unnecessary energy. Second, I'm going to knock people off balance in such a way that it puts them on the defensive, making it less likely for me to get done what I need to get done in the future. Third, somehow, someway, my behavior will catch up with me. It never fails. It may be a week, a month, or a year later, but somehow you pay for being an asshole.

But if I enter a similar situation from a place of active humility, I'll get what I want without any negative consequences. If I know that I'm deserving, but not entitled, I'll be that much more of a success. Look at Dr. Martin Luther King

Jr. He was humble, he did not retaliate, and as a result, he made huge strides in the civil rights struggle. Let's take a quick look at the Israeli-Palestinian conflict. Violence met with violence, the cruelty ante being upped for years, and where have they gotten? People dead on both sides, and they're still not any closer to a resolution. Humility is a trip.

When I first met my wife, I was good. I had a decent job, money in the bank, and a great social life. I had real friends, not just some random acquaintances. And I developed a relationship with myself that resulted in a healthy personality. I felt complete. I was still committed to my personal development, but life was good. Well, everything was good except that I had no one to *share* this with.

I felt that I deserved a mate—not was entitled to but deserving of. Let me tell you what an eye-opening experience that was. DLM #6. There is no better feeling than being so at ease with yourself, so comfortable with your existence that you can be vulnerable enough to accept a lover into your life on equal terms. This was how I came to be with my wife. I took my head out of my ass, accepted who I was, faults and all, and gave it to her raw. "This is who I am." And things couldn't be better. Needless to say there were things that we discovered about each other that freaked us both out, but that's how it is. We accepted it, worked through it, and then moved on to the bigger and better.

One of the spookiest things I have ever heard is that people need to be with someone so they can feel complete. What type of logic is that? If you are an incomplete person, most likely, you'll attract only incomplete people. Two half people walking around, looking at the world in an incomplete way— it just doesn't cut it.

What grade do you get if you don't turn in all of your assignments? Incomplete. What happens if you send in some paperwork and you forgot to sign a crucial section? It is sent back to you because it was incomplete. That isn't something to base a relationship on. Before inviting someone to share your life, be sure that you have a complete life worth sharing.

Rifle through and arrange your personal baggage before inviting someone to be a part of your life. Try to find who you truly are instead of what society and social pressures dictate. It is so much easier to talk about it than to do it. Trust me. I am in my thirties and am only now beginning to fully understand what this means. And that is OK. I can finally be fine with it. Back in the day, I would have adopted another persona to cope with my lack of self-awareness, or I would have hurt someone's feelings to make myself feel better. Thankfully, those days are over.

It would be wonderful if our society were amenable to men being something other than what is traditionally held up as being a man. But society won't give it to us, so we must carve out our own spaces. By doing this, we will become more connected than we have ever been.

Heart of Darkness

We are always being told to hate ourselves. If you don't have the right car, you ain't shit. Don't have the right clothes? You ain't shit. You don't own the latest "it" thing? You might as well kill yourself.

Television commercials, "lifestyle" magazines, and movies all inform us that we will never be as cool as the actor sitting on top of the (rented) kick-ass car, drinking the best drink, and keeping company with the hottest woman. There is no way that our egos can abide this, so we try to become that actor or musician or athlete. Most of us would break our necks if we could be just that much cooler in the eyes of the general public.

Take all of this pressure, and now add race to the mix—things can become almost unbearable. While most men will never live up to the images projected of them, most men of color don't even exist in the eyes of the general populace. And if we do, the image is always manipulated to serve some industry's interest. Basically, people of color are portrayed in negative or stereotyped images that are more urban mascot or corporate shill than human being.

If you are Asian/Pacific Islander, for example, you are barely even represented in this country. The best API representations are on *Lost, Heroes*, and *Battlestar Galactica*. This pisses off a lot of my Asian friends, but I tell them to be thankful. When they ask why, I tell them to look at how images of black men have been tainted and ask them if they would want to be in the same boat. My Native American brothers also don't exist, except for the wooden Indian statue holding a handful of cigars or as some sports team logo. Much respect to the author Sherman Alexie for making himself and his people known, but damn! Where are you, brothers? As I write this, America is still in Iraq. The images of my Middle Eastern homeboys are being used to promote hatred. Men of color never control their own images. The awful thing about this is that most of us, especially black men, will try to adopt or accept the corrupted images of ourselves.

Brothers are the first in line to parrot the lowest common denominators of our race. For example, let's touch upon this renewed and vigorous appreciation (lust) for jewelry. Diamonds, platinum, and white and red gold adorn the watches, teeth, lawn mowers, and toasters of rappers and athletes. If it has a blank surface, one of these silly fucks is going to find someone to stick a precious metal or stone on it. In the case of rappers, most rational folks understand that all of the jewelry, cars, and women are rented for the music videos, television programs, awards shows, and so on. The problem is that some young, impressionable, and violently poor men of color either don't know this or choose to ignore the facts.

These youngsters look at these videos not as entertainment but as a road map to heaven. The young men I have spoken with seem to think that getting a bunch of stuff will elevate them out of their nasty situations. When I asked them how jewels and rims on cars could help them, they couldn't come up with any answers. They just told me to "stop hatin'." Some of them even insulted and threatened me. Interesting, to say the least. The pure resistance that I receive when talking with these young men is a prime example of how black folks have allowed this society to keep us down. Make no mistake, we allow the machine to keep rolling along. Hell, most of us are happy to be the grease.

Maybe I get so down on my own because I have always been the anomaly. I hated sports and wasn't too concerned with pursuing women until later in my life. Growing up I listened to 1980s new wave, ska, punk, and hip-hop, plus I played endless hours of role-playing games. All of this contributed to my being semi-ostracized by black men. But the capper, I believe, was the fact that I "talked white." And I think this is the main reason that most of these young men don't take me as seriously as they should. In a roundabout way, this makes a little sense.

Being black and educated is a semi-amusing curiosity to white folks but an undesirable way of life for many black folks. This is why most of us will never rise above the despair in which a disproportionate number of us dwell. We just don't believe it is possible for us to rise above our current misery. Most of us have lost the ability to hope.

And that ability is an easy thing to lose—because the more we hope, the more we get let down. Our dreams become these little nuggets that are just out of our reach. Being black in this country breeds a damn near hostage mentality. We're like those women who stick around even though their men are beating the hell out of them. Everyone knows what's going on, everyone sees the abuse, but there we stay, nursing our wounds, huddling in corners, and hoping that the beatings will stop, and "he" will see us as we truly are: beautiful.

It's sort of difficult to love yourself in situations like this. So we stop hoping, stop dreaming, and either become totally complacent or try to rewrite the rules in our favor. But you can't rewrite rules if you aren't considered an equal player.

We form gangs to replace the absent male energy in our lives. Some of us figure that fame is the ticket, so we spend our time trying to escape from who we are in order to become icons. When you become an icon, skin color doesn't matter. You can go where you want, and the only question you will be asked is "Can I have your autograph?"

The thing about fame is that a lot of us don't care how we attain it. We'll even kill for it. Why should a kid care about the consequences of shooting someone? If he goes to jail, he will be known as a stone-cold killer and will be able to parlay that into social currency, making a name for himself. If he doesn't get caught, he'll have more street cred than he knows what to do with.

We go through all of this and more, just to carve out a place for ourselves in this world, a place where we can feel comfortable. We go through the hard work of rearranging ourselves so that the world will accept us, but most of the general populace couldn't care less. The rest of the populace either copies or uses us to further their financial, cultural, and psychic prosperity.

If it weren't for black American culture, popular culture as we know it would not exist. If Elvis Presley had never been exposed to black folks, white America's collective pelvis would probably still be frozen. Folks would be square dancing their asses off. It seems that every publicly successful Caucasian has to bastardize (or pay disingenuous homage to) some element of black culture to legitimize his or her I'm-so-hip quotient. The list is quite extensive, but here is just a taste.

Warren Beatty, *Bulworth*
Jamie Kennedy, *Malibu's Most Wanted* and *Blowin' Up*
Steve Martin, *Bringin' Down the House*
Kevin Smith, *Dogma*, *Chasing Amy*
Quentin Tarantino, *Pulp Fiction*, *Jackie Brown*
Lisa Kudrow, *Marci X*
Bloodhound Gang, everything they've ever done or said
MTV, and all of its related programming
Bomb-itty of Errors, the worst thing I have ever seen
The prevalent use of the silly term *bling bling* among
     suburban residents
Eric Clapton
The Beatles, but they were so great, so they get a pass
Britney Spears
Christina Aguilera, in her "Dirrty" phase
Shaun of the Dead
George W. Bush, Condi, and Colin gettin' jiggy wit' it
Justin Timberlake, a wholesale Michael Jackson rip-off
Michael Bolton, what he did to the Isleys is unforgivable

The above is only a small listing of how black folks have been robbed, imitated, and otherwise used as tools for white liberation. Now I want to take it to the next level. I can understand why folks would want to emulate black culture—the oppressed is always much cooler than the oppressor, so it makes a certain kind of sense that people would want to align themselves with the downtrodden. But the thing that gets me is how far people are willing to go to become part of the culture. Before I get into all of that, I would like to clarify my point. Not apologize for, but clarify.

As far as I'm concerned, culture is kind of like the forest. Come visit, have some fun, and experience something that you've never experienced before, but don't take or leave a damn molecule. It is not your place to do so. Many people participate in black culture, but they know their place. They know that they are guests. I have been involved in Asian martial arts for the past twenty-odd years, and I still consider myself a guest. I'm not going to go adding, subtracting, or changing things in the art without first getting some sort of positive consensus that it is OK to do so. And even if I did get the thumbs-up, I'd be hesitant because this isn't mine. By my instructor's good graces, I am allowed to practice and teach the art. And I know that I will never become Chinese, Japanese, or Filipino through osmosis. So please take this as a lesson. No matter how much hip-hop you listen to, no matter how many Ecko, Phat Farm, Baby Phat, or Sean John outfits you own, no matter how many black folks you fuck, you will never *be* black. Doesn't work that way. Sorry.

The cultural divisions in our society spring from our unwillingness to accept different cultures at face value. When we encounter something new and unfamiliar, we immediately label it so that we can understand it. We quantify and categorize this "other" so that we can feel better about our interactions; we do this so that we can have the upper hand in order to gain some sort of superior foothold over this new "it." It makes us feel comfortable; it puts us at ease when we do this. If we can't easily toss it in a convenient category, we will change the properties of it to better suit our purposes. So black folks become criminals and Asians become asexual human calculators and Latinos become lazy border hoppers (which seems to be oxymoronic) and Arabs become terrorists and on and on and on.

I can't tell you how many times that this has come up and people whine, "I don't have a culture. I'm an American." We are all Americans, but American culture is sometimes good for only one thing: oppressing a group so much that beautiful art is created. Hip-hop, jazz, blues, soul, and gospel music are prime examples of this. It's like we are all pieces of coal, and the pressure that America exerts on us turns us into diamonds. And sometimes this American pressure cooker forces us to look back to our ancestry.

I wasn't the biggest fan of my generation's back-to-Africa movement. I felt that I was born here, and I felt I was entitled to what this country had to offer. My mistake. There was nothing here for me culturally, so I began to investigate my Puerto Rican and Caribbean roots, and a whole other world opened up. Half of getting to know and being comfortable with yourself is getting to know and becoming comfortable with your ancestors. This isn't some left-of-center metaphysics; this is how I truly feel. But most (mainly younger) folks would rather look into stylized blackness than into their own histories. You can come and play but don't even think about taking over.

I have been witnessing an extremely disturbing trend lately. This trend seems to apply to only an aspect of black culture: hip-hop. Young people are calling each other "nigger." You can't walk down the street these days without hearing the *nigger* bomb dropped from all angles. A lot of my brothers and sisters use the word as a term of endearment, but I do not. The word has so much hate attached to it that it is beyond reclamation. But try explaining this to the black folks and others who use it in a "nonracist" way, and they'll make every excuse to cling to their *nigger* lifeboat.

About a year ago I went to Chinatown to grab something to eat. I wasn't trying to appropriate anyone's culture—just hungry, and Chinatown was within walking distance. As I walked past this little bakery, I was attacked by the most incredible smell. My stomach responded loudly, so I went into the joint with the full intention of spending an obscene amount of money on barbecued chicken buns, dumplings, and other pastries. Through my hunger fog, I heard some music. Upon further concentration, I pinpointed the Jay-Z track that spilled out of the little red-curtained back room. Stepping to the counter, I looked at the walls, and it struck me as funny that I was hearing Jay-Z's flow and looking at all sorts of Chinese statuary and whatnot. The veil between cultures is growing thinner with each passing year.

I waited for a couple of minutes, and then *he* entered, accompanied by a Cheech and Chong–sized cloud of marijuana smoke. He of the Chinese-character-tattooed arms and neck. He of the pants hanging way off his ass, exposing his boxers to the world. He of the XXX white T-shirt, NBA baseball cap, and two cellular phones clipped directly to his underwear. It was him: the twenty-first-century homeboy. If the sight of him gave me pause, the sound of him froze me in my tracks.

"Yo! What up, nigga? What you want?"

Straight-up deer-in-the-headlights time. I had to look around the place to check to see if he was speaking to someone else. Did this cat just call me a "nigger"? He couldn't have. I had to make sure.

"Excuse me?"

"What you want, nigga? I got it all."

I don't even have to tell you how in shock I was. All I was trying to do was get something to eat, but now I had to enter into the part of the black American existence that I hate: the role of the cultural educator. I scanned my mental file cabinets, hoping to find less volatile words than the ones I wanted to use.

Let me tell you, it took some doing, but I felt that I knew just what to say. I had two missions that needed to be accomplished. The first was to reeducate this cat against using the word in any context. The second was to let go of some of the anger I was feeling.

"Yo, man. That word is not cool to use. On any other day, you and me would be brawling right now, but I'ma chalk it up to you not knowing any better. So, from this point forward, you need to stop saying 'nigger,' 'nigga,' 'nizzle,' or any variation of the word. It is offensive and has a whole history of pain for my people. I came in here treating you with respect, and you should treat me the same way."

There, I told him. I gave him just enough of a threat, mixed with a clear explanation and just a hint of "treat others as you want to be treated" tossed in there at the end. There is no way in hell that this dude could argue against what I said. Or so I thought.

"Damn, nigga. Why are you so sensitive? All I was tryna do is make you feel welcome, and you gonna threaten me? Nigga, please. You want something or what, nigga?"

"What did I just tell you about using that word?"

"Jay-Z say it! Right? Jay-Z say it. If he can say it, I can say it," he said.

The power of his conviction was fairly impressive. It was time to switch tactics. It was now time for the do-unto-others remix. I have used the remix, with much success, numerous times, and I was damned sure that it could work here. Without any thought to the repercussions, I gave it to him.

"All right, you non-jazz-playing, left-turn-from-the-right-turn-lane, not-one-of-your-women-have-their-natural-hair-color, dog-eating gook. Let me get three chicken dumplings, a steamed bun, and an eggroll, you slant-eyed sonuvabitch!"

This Negro simulacrum had the nerve, the sheer audacity, to get mad at me.

"How are you going to come up in my place and dog me out like that? That's fucked up. I showed you kindness, and you dis me? Fuck you, nigga. If I were you, I'd leave and never come back to the C.T."

There was a decision to be made. Do I stay and try to explain my point, or do I realize that I am in Chinatown and home is far, far away and get to steppin'?

While safely at home, I thought about the ignorant cultural exchange that took place less than a half hour prior. A couple of things left me cold, and I still haven't reconciled them. Not one bit of good came out of that verbal volley—nothing whatsoever.

I was disgusted with him for not being able to see that he was way out of line, that he was completely wrong. But more than that, I was disgusted with myself. How in the hell did I come up with those words? Was I more of a bigot than I thought? Am I living a lie, only pretending to be some ethno-cultural crusader, when in fact I was just as bad as the people I try to put in check? Or, on the flip side, was I just defending myself and my people? I'm still trying to figure out all of that shit. I haven't come any closer to an answer, though.

I guess it is obvious that the word *nigger* bothers me. The disgusting part is that I'm one of a rapidly shrinking number of black folks who find the word disgusting. Every time I hear that word, or one of its many derivatives, pictures of lynchings, cross burnings, and beatings by the police invade my consciousness.

It's as if the word *nigger* is an unlimited run of trading cards: "I'll give you two Nigger Bitches for one Dumb Nigger and two Niggaz. Collect all 100,000!"

Folks who don't deal with race or color in their daily lives (most white people and sellouts) try to convince the world and themselves that *race is no longer a factor in this country*. And that the use of *nigger* is just a semi-embarrassing colloquialism: *nigger* as the new "man" or "dude" or "homeboy."

If it is no longer a factor, why is it that so many black folks, and in my experience men in particular, feel so utterly dehumanized when this word is hurled in our direction like a little low self-esteem grenade? The shit explodes, and we begin to doubt ourselves—thinking that we are the lowest of the low. It is no fun being hated or mistrusted because of something like skin color. If you want to hate me, hate me for my politics, my taste in clothes and music, how I call women "sweetheart" (whether I know them or not)—hate me for anything other than my enhanced melanin. And get *nigger* out of your mouths. You too, black folks. This is one word that cannot be reclaimed. All we have done is open the door of its use to every other culture on the planet, and then when one of us calls them on it, you'll hear back "Well, you say it." Leave it alone.

You have been warned.

A Nigger by Any Other Name

Africoon

Antique Farm Equipment

Billy Reuben (the pigment that makes feces brown is called bilirubin)

Black Apples (because we hang from trees)

Blackie

Blue Gummer

Boogie (like the monster from bedtime stories)

Bootlick

Brillo Pad

Brownie

Buck

Bumper Lips

Burnt Match

Chain Dragger

Chicken Bandit

Coon

Coontang (black women)

Crime Stopper (a black woman who has an abortion)

Darkie

Future Inmate

Gorilla

Half-Human

Jigaboo

Lawn Jockey

Lincoln's Mistake

Mammy

Midnight

Monkey

Moolie

Mud People

Oil Slick

Oreo
Pickaninny
Property
Roach (they come out at night
  to raise hell; turn on the [pol-
  ice] lights and they scatter)
Rope Neck
Schwarze (German for the
  word *black* and derogatory
  Yiddish slang)
Shadow
Smoke
Smokey
Spook
Tar Baby
Tree Ornament
Tree Swinger
Velcro Head
Welfare Monkey
Wind Chime

Fucked up, ain't it? The worst thing about it is that I showed this list to one of my friends and she gave me a different list that was twice as long.

Damn!

The Dark Side

It is a shame that for the rest of my life I will associate the word *nigger* with the *Star Wars* universe. It was 1977, and by the time I got into kindergarten that year, I had seen George Lucas's epic five times. It was everything a little boy could want: spaceships, laser guns, wizards, and robots.

I'm not sure about you, but the kids at my school always wanted to pretend to be the characters in whatever movie or television show was popular at the time. So that autumn, all we heard at recess was "Let's play *Star Wars*." I always wanted to play, but I used my recess time to read comic books and to daydream. Rarely did I hang out with other kids.

The weekend of my second week of kindergarten, my mother took my uncle and me to see the film again. It was different this time. I was no longer a voyeur; I was a participant! I was Han Solo. By this time, I had already shown that I had criminal leanings, so Mr. Solo was the perfect choice.

Monday's recess time came around, and this time I was ready to get my *Star Wars* on. I stood in line to get picked as Matthew May began to assign people to their respective characters.

"Okay, Bobby, you can be Luke Skywalker. Tia, you're Princess Leia. Nick and Mike, you're twins, so you can be R2-D2 and C-3PO. And I'm always Han Solo." He looked at me, his face one big knot of confusion, "Um, Shawn. Um, well, you're a nigger, so you can be either Chewbacca or Dark Vader." Dark Vader, mind you, not Darth.

Matthew had just called me a nigger. It wasn't like I was a stranger to the word. I heard it several times a day in my neighborhood. Everyone used it.

"What's up, nigger?"

"You know, nigger. Just coolin'."

"That nigger is crazy as a motherfucker!"

But that was black folks saying it with an undercurrent of affection, so I never thought that anything was wrong with it. It was a fact of ghetto life.

This was the first time that I had ever heard a white person say it. And it was directed at me, with no affection whatsoever. Needless to say, for reasons I didn't understand back then, I felt like shit.

So my choices were either to be a big, furry, unintelligible dog-man or to be the biggest, baddest, blackest source of evil in the entire galaxy. As you might have guessed, the choice wasn't difficult at all. "I'll be *Darth* Vader." With that choice, I turned myself into a double minority: I was the only black kid playing *Star Wars*, and I was the only villain. There were no storm troopers around to conveniently absorb the onslaught of rebel hostilities. My aunt had always told me that no matter what I did or where I was, I should always have backup or a weapon close at hand. It was five against one, and I wasn't a real big fan of those odds. Not to mention that I was drowning in a ball of confusion and haywire emotions because of Matthew's "nigger" barb, which rolled so easily off his tongue. I searched the ground and then the sky looking for answers, looking for a way to even the odds. In truth, I was also hoping to find a name for what I was going through at that moment, but five-year-old minds and spirits aren't ready to handle concepts of this nature. And then, *pow*, an epiphany! A gift from the cosmos landed, ever so lightly, in the forefront of my consciousness. It was on! I headed back to the school building. Matthew blocked my passage.

"Where are you going?"

"I need to get into character," I told him. (It was something like that. It was thirty years ago, so I can't recall all of the particulars.) The Darth Vader wheeze corrupted my thoughts.

I continued my march to my homeroom, and right there, on the blackboard's chalk tray, I saw what I needed: a yardstick. Armed and feeling empowered, I strolled back to the playground. My classmates were already in the middle of a heated game when Bobby Andersen pointed at me and yelled at the top of his asthmatic lungs, "There's Dark Vader! Get him!" I remember it like it was yesterday. A herd of white kids bounded off the jungle gym and began to rush toward me. Why they didn't notice—or comment on—the yardstick that I was holding was beyond me.

"You puny rebels don't stand a chance against me," I said in the most sinister, breathy voice that I could muster. Bobby came into range first. Making the appropriate light saber noise, I clocked him right upside his head. He was down for the count, a goose egg already beginning to form. Tia got it in the knees and ankles. I was a child possessed! You should have seen me. The twins, Nick and Mike, caught it in the nose and the right arm, respectively. All that was left was Matthew's "nigger"-callin' ass. Mind you, I still didn't know why I was mad. I just knew that he had to get his ass whipped. It was his destiny.

I stalked him all around the play area. In the back of my young mind, I was wondering why none of the teachers saw this and tried to stop me. I guess fortune had my back. Finally, I backed him into a corner. He tried to say something, but with the blood rushing in my ears and the hurt in my heart, I could not make it out. Then I just unloaded on him. Whack! Whack! Whack! Just as it was starting to get good to me, the enormous Miss Myonovich grabbed me, snatched the yard-stick from my hand, and slammed me to the ground. "What is going on here?" she asked with her thick Yugoslavian accent.

Just then, all of the kids I had attacked came gimping up to us, looking like *Night of the Living Dead* mini-me's. Ever the leader, Matthew decided that he would speak for the entire group of injured five-year-olds. "He just went crazy and beat us," he said. His crew all nodded in agreement.

"And what do you have to say for yourself, Mr. Taylor?" Teacher "the Hutt" questioned, not caring about what excuse I was about to give.

The tears were at the front door, ready to exit, but I couldn't let them go. You see, in my neighborhood real men didn't cry. So I sucked it up and told her why I went off on their asses.

"He called me a 'nigger,' Miss M.! And I didn't like it!" I said this with as much sorrow as possible.

"Is this true, Mr. May?" she asked him, probably knowing it was true but not wanting to believe it, or not caring either way.

Matthew, as bold as headline news, said, "Unh-unh. He's a liar, and God hates liars."

The beat-to-hell *Star Wars* group chimed in, labeling me the liar that I wasn't then but would become later. Miss Myonovich lost her ever-lovin' mind.

"How dare you lie on this boy? You are a nasty little thing. I'm taking you to the principal's office!"

She snatched me by my Geranimals and dragged me to the office of the most evil person in the entire galaxy. More evil than even Darth Vader, Principal Byrd was the living embodiment of every kindergartner's nightmares. He was around six foot three but couldn't have weighed more than 120 or 130. His skin was a white and orange combination, kind of like a demented, anthropomorphic Dreamsicle.

Miss M. relayed the story to him, conveniently leaving out the part of Matthew's calling me a "nigger," and left me alone to deal with He Who Frightens Little Kids.

One, two, three elongated minutes later, he finally spoke. (You're a damn fool if you thought that I was going to break the silence first. I was terrified.)

"Shawn," he used my first name. He *always* called kids by their surnames. I must have been about to get into super trouble, I thought. "What on earth were you thinking about, attacking your classmates?" His breath smelled of cigars and old, hot cheese.

"Matthew called me a 'nigger.'"

"Miss Myonovich didn't say anything about that."

"Well, it's true."

"Are you calling Miss Myonovich a liar?"

"No, but that's what he called me."

"And?"

And. Now how fucked up was that? There I was, dealing with my first taste of prejudice, and this guy says, "and?" I just stared at him; the seed of my own prejudice had just been sown.

"He hurt my feelings."

"Are you going to hit everyone in your life who hurts your feelings?" he asked. He then stood and slithered toward me. He put his hands on the arms of the chair that I was sitting in, knelt down, leaned in, and said something that shattered what little ego I had left. "Know your place."

Without another word to me, he called my mother and informed her that she had to come and get me right then and keep me out of school for a day because of my behavior. Suspended as a kindergartner. That's a damn shame. Of course, he omitted the fact that I was called a "nigger." After speaking with my mother, he waved his hand and shooed me out of his office. As I was waiting for my mom, all of these emotions were rippling through me. I was mad, sad, and confused all at the same time. When my mom arrived, let's just say that she was a little south of happy.

Let me tell you a couple of things to put all of this into perspective. My mom was newly divorced. We had next to no money, and we weren't getting any type of child support, so she was a bit bitter at anything having to do with my father. Since I was my father's son, she didn't have much use for me at all. We had no car, so she had to take a long-ass bus ride to come retrieve me. And, on top of all this, she really wanted to be white. Well, that isn't terribly accurate. She just wanted to seamlessly fit into white society, maybe even find herself a white man, with a decent-sized bank account, who would sweep all of her troubles away with a couple of well-placed dollars. Having a maniacal chocolate chip of a son who was suspended from school in kindergarten was not in her plans. I was a dead man.

I told her my side of the story. Hell, I told her three different versions of my side of the story. But she just wasn't having it. If spanking a child were a sport, my mom would have been the MVP of ass whoopings. She beat me with such glee that I thought she would never stop. She beat me until her arm grew tired, and then she sent me off to my room. I got in fights all the time on the block, and she never got that mad. Well, I never used yardsticks in them either, but still. Little did I know that my mom was dealing with an unchecked mental and physical illness for almost her entire life. But back then I labeled her *enemy*.

My mother was one for passive survival, and she felt that the only way black folks—no matter which part of the diaspora they hailed from—could make it in America was to shut up and stay below the societal radar. In her mind, the less we were seen or heard, the better our chances of existing unmolested. I felt that this was a coward's logic, and it made me dislike her even more.

I spent my day off doing what any other wronged person would have—I plotted my revenge (never went through with it, though). I also made an impossible pact with myself that I would never see another *Star Wars* film.

At the time, I didn't even know that more episodes were coming out, but what the hell. Three years later, *The Empire Strikes Back* descended on movie screens all across America, and I was first in line. To this day, I love the hell out of that movie. Although he had an intergalactic perm, Lando Calrissian was the man! He was even working in concert with Darth Vader, betraying the intrepid heroes. All right! Justice, after a fashion.

Now, I'm not trying to say that it was *Star Wars* or George Lucas who activated Matthew's prejudice, nor am I saying that I blame them for the wave of racism I felt through the rest of the 1970s and then on into the '80s and beyond. All I'm saying is that I feel a wee bit cheated that most of the people of my generation can, and do, bond over the *Star Wars* flicks. I can't even recall a scene without stoking the little belly-fire of rage that I have been trying (and failing) to suppress since I was a child.

So, fuck *Star Wars*.

Long live *Star Trek*!

WGBs

Aside from the bags of Hershey's Miniatures candies that I could never afford as a kid, there was one other thing—technically, two things—that I longed for: White Girl Boobies (WGBs). Man. I can't even tell you how many times I fantasized about what lurked underneath the sweaters of white girls. I was no stranger to the sight of boobies, but there was something magical, maybe even quasi-spiritual, about them.

By this time, I had seen boobies of all shapes, sizes, and colors, usually with tattoos, stretch marks, scars, and/or babies attached to them. Puerto Rican, Caribbean, African American, Cuban, and a host of multiethnic boobies were always bouncing around my neighborhood, and I never really paid them any mind. I was under the misguided impression that the boobies of dark women were functional, had specific tasks to perform, but White Girl Boobies were something else entirely. Kind of like museum pieces, you know, works of art.

Was it conditioning? Damn right. The only station that we received was PBS, so I was always seeing shows where Dark Girl Boobies from Dark Continents flapped and hung all over the place. But you never saw WGBs on those programs. This intrigued me. If I had had cable, it would have been a different story, but I didn't, so there. I was on some Indiana Jones shit when I made my plans to discover the secrets of the WGBs.

I wasn't going straight for the boobies just then; I needed a map to the hidden treasure, a blueprint as to what I might find once the upper parts of the clothing were removed. Mind you, I was just a preteen, but I was at the dawn of my horniness. One day I was playing with action figures, and the next I was playing with my dick. Strange.

I didn't even know what sex was back then. All I knew was that every time I imagined those beautiful swells that hitchhiked on the front of Caucasian females, I built a little pup tent in my Underoos.

There was this little bodega a block from my house, and it had an enormous selection of nudie magazines. All of the mags with dark women were unbagged and readily available to be pawed through. All of the *Playboys*, *Penthouses*, and the like were behind the counter, were polybagged, and had that strategic cardboard placed right at breast level. That was some frustrating but nonetheless enticing shit. All of the kids used to rob the hell out of the place. Sugar Babies here, a pack of Now and Laters there—we were out of control. I was about to up the ante. Petty larceny was the birthright of every project-born child. So was porn.

My curiosity, my hunger, my desire for WGBs was so intense that I didn't have the wherewithal to come up with a sensible plan. This had to be a strictly smash-and-grab job. I wasn't so far gone that I didn't take at least a couple of precautions. The grabbing would be easy; it was the getting out of the market and safely away that was proving to be the most difficult part of this operation. But I had an idea.

I spent fifty precious cents and bought two tiny cars from those red-painted vending machines that squat near the doors of every supermarket in America. Immediately tossing the little Trans Ams in the trash, I carefully put the plastic egglike containers in my Wrangler pockets and dashed home. Being on welfare had its advantages, because almost every item of food we received was some industrial, family-sized shit. So when I filled those two containers with black pepper right to the rim, my mother would never know that I was using our commodities for purposes other than eating. Now that I had my defensive measures taken care of, there was nothing left for me to do but execute the mission.

The walk to the bodega was filled with exhilaration and a sense of dread. What if I were caught? Would they put me in jail? It didn't matter; risks needed to be taken if one wanted to gain knowledge. So I pressed on, more determined than ever to solve the mystery of what caused my almost constant erection. If I didn't get to the bottom of it soon, I might lose my mind.

In all my life, I don't think an event has transpired as fast as when I stole that magazine. At the entrance to the store, on the left side of the doorway, there was a group of newspaper racks, half empty, adjacent to the counter. Farther left, up and behind the counter and about as tall as a man, is where the mother lode was. Dozens of plastic bag–covered nudie magazines hung like little fruits on a spray-painted iron tree, ready to be plucked and devoured. If someone as tall as my eleven-year-old self stood on the news rack nearest the door, he could stick his skinny arm through the gap of the Plexiglas partition, reach an issue of *Gallery* magazine, and be out the door before he was noticed. That's the way I had envisioned it, and that was how it was going to go down.

Taking a couple of short, sharp breaths to psych myself up for the job at hand, I ran into the store, stood on the rack, snaked my arm through the gap, snatched the magazine, and felt a sudden rush of elation course through my body. But then the unthinkable happened. My seventy-pound frame was too much for the rack, and the whole thing collapsed. It couldn't just collapse either. It had to make more noise than a fleet of DC-10s. As I was falling, I hadn't pulled my arm back fast enough, so my arm was caught between the wall and the sheet of Plexiglas.

There I was, my left arm all sliced up and bloody, holding a porn magazine, the rest of my body folded in some awkward yogalike position amid a broken news rack, buried beneath a population of *AutoTrader* papers. Oh yeah, and the cashier was coming at top speed! When he rounded the corner and was about four feet in front of me, I reached in my pocket and conjured one of the pepper bombs that I had made earlier. I visualized the parabola needed to make the bomb land on his face and blind him so I could escape. The bomb was tossed, and it landed expertly on his forehead, bounced off, and landed on the hard concrete floor of the bodega, intact and with not a scratch on it. Oh, damn, I had forgotten to take the tape off! I had taped the lid to the bowl part of the egg so it wouldn't break open in my pocket. That would teach me about being too careful.

The cashier, shocked to high heaven, picked up my device, turned it over in his hands, and freaked the fuck out. "You, boy. You trying to make me sneeze? You steal from me, and then you want to make me sneeze? You're gonna get it now!"

Thinking to myself that I didn't want to be one of those kids who had to go through the Scared Straight program, I braced myself and, with superhuman strength, yanked my arm free. The sound was awful. I left bits of my skin and blood all over the place. That was one of the worst pains I had ever felt. It was the type of pain that made you almost piss yourself. Not quite, but some liquid was at the pee-pee hole. I was so stunned that I was free, I was almost caught until I snapped to and booked it out of there.

The cashier was determined but chubby, so there was no chance he would catch me in a straightaway. I grabbed my last pepper bomb, this time remembering to take the tape off, and I threw it at my pursuer. My aim was on point again, and the bomb did what it was supposed to do—it exploded right in his eyes. "I wasn't trying to make you sneeze, you fat punk! I was trying to blind you." In retrospect, that was a fucked-up thing to do, but back in the day it was funny as hell. I can still see him sputtering, wiping his eyes, and making threats to introduce my penis to a pair of vise grips, some salt, and some sandpaper. Funny.

There was a double high racing through my body, a high from the adrenaline rush and one from the thrill of knowing that my curiosity was about to be sated. Booking it to my hiding place (an unused janitor's storage room in the basement of a neighboring building), I turned the viewing of the White Girl Boobies into a ritualistic event. Taking a broken-handled broom, I swept away piles of garbage, giving myself a semiclean space to get down in. When this holy task was completed, I reverently placed the magazine on the floor. I inspected my treasure for the first time, and damn it, there was a black bar printed on the bag itself, right over the naughty bits. The anticipation was about to cause me to develop an ulcer.

Plastic bags on porno magazines are difficult to open, especially when your hands are sweating and trembling with desire. I finally removed the bag but was stymied again. OK, now this shit was getting on my nerves. The woman on the cover was wearing a swimsuit. Would I ever get to see the boobies?

I opened the magazine, and (insert devotional music here) I saw the White Girl Boobies. Both of them. They didn't have tattoos, stretch marks, or scars, and there wasn't any milk dripping out the nipple either. I was in love. Well, maybe not love, but I definitely liked those pale, perfect little snow globes. My tiny penis dug the boobies, too. Man, I wish I had known how to masturbate back then because I could have gotten more pleasure from my ill-gotten, self-taught anatomy lesson before the gang that used the janitor's closet as a meeting place caught me and stole my stolen magazine.

That situation was beyond humiliating—it was terrifying. I was prey in the middle of a circle of predators, and I had something we both wanted.

"Look at that little nigger; he a freak!"

"What you got there, B?"

"Yo, nigger. That's a titty mag. Hand it over, B."

I couldn't say anything to them. My eyes were focused on, hell, hypnotized by, the flaming skulls that these guys had on their jackets and vests. Intellectually, I knew that every human had a skull, but when that skull is grinning and surrounded by flames, it is not cool. One of the skull bearers made a play for the magazine; I pulled it back from him and then leapt back, striking a stance that I had learned in my YMCA karate class. Everyone but me burst into fits of laughter.

"You a fast little nigger, I'll give you that. Just give us that magazine and get the fuck out of here."

"No."

"No? Are you out of your mind? Get him!"

That shit was over in less than a heartbeat. I think that I got off one kick before the dark-skinned, denim, and flaming-skull avalanche enveloped me.

I woke up on top of one of the dryers in the laundry room. My busted lip, my bloody nose, and my swollen right eye made beautiful companion pieces to my already damaged left arm. But I had seen the WGBs, and the pain was worth it.

When I got home, I told my mom that I was jumped by some kids for no reason and went straight to my room. Taking out a sheet of paper and a flesh-colored crayon, I tried to re-create the boobies and record them for posterity because I didn't know when I would see any again. The women's in the magazines was even paler than that crayon, but I pressed on. When I was finished, two squiggly circles with two dots in the middle of each adorned the paper. I checked my pants, but I wasn't nearly as excited about them as I was before. Maybe it was the pain. Maybe I could get excited about only the real thing, or maybe I knew I was too young to be worrying about boobies.

Nah, no one is too young to dig on boobies.

I folded the paper and placed it under my pillow. It worked for teeth, why couldn't it work for boobies? As I lay in bed, I wondered when I would see White Girl Boobies again. Did it matter? I had seen them once; wasn't that enough? I began to fall asleep, attempting to conjure that blonde-haired, blue-eyed woman and her glorious breasts. My mental eye moved from her head down her wonderful chest (lingering there a moment) and then followed the curve of her stomach, right down to her coochie.

Now, what in God's name was that? I hadn't ever seen anything like that before. The coochie didn't make me lustful like the boobies did. In fact, the coochie kind of scared me. And it continued to scare me until my first year of college.

This makes me look as if I'm one of those people I despise, doesn't it? Let me put it into context.

Normally I hate to explain anything that I write or perform, but every person who read this told me that I needed to explain the point of it. Some claimed that this story was just a reverse-exoticism story, and those people are partially right. Others stated that all I did was demonize women of color, render their sexuality null and void. Point taken.

My aim was to illustrate that even at so young an age I was taught that women of color were not to be desired. And I wasn't the only young, ghetto, male child who felt that way.

Hell, I remember this pimp telling me, "Nigger broads are for fucking, at home, and white bitches are for going out in public. If you got a white bitch on your arm, you get to go places that you ain't never even thought of. For real, little nigger. Fancy-ass restaurants and shit."

I'll be very candid with you—it took me a long time to find women of color desirable. Let me stop lying; it took me a long time to find black women desirable. All of the anti–black female spin that I was exposed to did its job. They were rarely in the movies or on television, and if they were, they were prostitutes or cleaners or receptionists. So I was fantasizing about *Wonder Woman*'s Lynda Carter when I should have been fantasizing about Jayne Kennedy and Beverly Johnson (if I could have known who they were back then).

My beautiful black sisters, mothers, aunties, and grand-mamas, please accept my apologies for not giving you your just due. You are all beautiful, and this story wasn't an attempt to discredit or belittle your beauty or sexuality. This was to show how misguided I was back in the day, and I want you all to know that I have regained my senses. Just ask my wife. I love you all.

Slower than a Speeding Bullet

Dying is one of those events that can only be classified as crazy. But the one thing that is even crazier than dying at eighteen years old is coming back from the dead. Not to say that I am Jesus, but I found myself an heir to the whole dying-and-rising-again thing. And to this day, nearly twenty years later, I'm still trying to wrap my head around the entire experience.

I used to love to dance. B-boying (break dancing) was my favorite thing to do. It was one of the few (legal) things that I was actually good at. When I battled people, they used to get so pissed at me. I wouldn't just dance against them; I'd take their moves and do them better. If not that, I'd mock the hell out of them. I'd get close enough to pull down their pants, or pretend that I was humping them, or after a knee-spin, I'd lift my leg like a dog and pretend to piss on their feet. I was a little bastard, but I was talented.

During one battle, I got more carried away than usual. This one dude and I were really going at it. The crowd was cheering, and I was on an obscene adrenaline high. Adulation and adrenaline are two of the main ingredients of stupidity. I swiped this dude's hat from his head, tossed it on the ground, stepped on it, and then used it as a spinning aid. I must have hit four or five revolutions before I stopped, arms folded across my chest, head tilted back in defiance. The "Oooohhhh" from the crowd made me smile deeply with self-satisfaction.

Without a backward glance, I walked away. A couple of my friends ran over to me, their mouths moving and arms waving frantically. I couldn't make out what they were saying, but I looked down and saw a pool of liquid at my feet, little droplets enlarging the pool by the minute. I followed the droplets to their source: me. One of my boys pointed to my gut. It looked like a chocolate jack-o-lantern spitting out strawberry sauce.

My crew tackled me to the ground, and I don't remember anything else until I woke up—and passed out again—in the back of an ambulance.

I had been shot. In the stomach. At point-blank range. And I died. I was daisy pushing for 150 seconds. And let me tell you, there were no welcoming lights or tunnels, and my life did not flash before my eyes. Death was like being surrounded by millions of televisions encased in Plexiglas with each screen showing clips of the *700 Club* with the volume turned way down. What I mean is that death is boring as fuck, and you are powerless to change your situation.

I had been face-to-face with my shooter, and I would have put money on the fact that the dude punched me. His arm drew back, then forward; I heard a dull "pop," and I felt the most excruciating pain in my midsection. Imagine a molten lava spider carousing in your stomach. Yeah, it hurt that bad. From fairly defined abdominal muscles to fertile ground for projectile incubation in no time flat.

So I'm chilling in the amber twilight of the afterworld when I feel this *tug*. I wasn't aware of having a body, but I felt my "self" being pulled somewhere. Then *pow!* I was reintroduced to the conscious world, right smack into my damaged and pain-wracked body. When I opened my eyes, a paramedic was smiling down at me. "A hundred fifty seconds, bro. You were gone for two and a half minutes. Dead. Welcome back."

As I was laying there, for some reason I kept thinking to myself that this is what it must feel like to be born. Oh yeah. Shit was bordering on the metaphysical. You see, I had been a C-section baby and was evicted before I had the chance to go out the front door, so I never had had to deal with the trauma of being born. I like to think that I escaped all of that pre- and postnatal stress. I feel that it was my bypass of birth pain that has caused me to go through so many trials. The following is, admittedly, a flawed and corny philosophy, but it acts as the touchstone for my psychosocial existence.

I have this theory that the Creator—whomever or whatever you wish it to be—makes us go through such traumatic births to humble us. The first thing we encounter when we are removed from the relative safety of our mother's womb is pain and displacement and sonic overload. It's a wonder that any of us make it past our initial twelve hours on this earth. Our inauspicious debuts should rein us in, no matter how subconsciously, ensuring that our egos don't run amok. But me being me, I was a little arrogant prick. Not arrogant in the sense that I felt I was above others but in the sense that I did not acknowledge that there would be any consequences for my actions.

I felt that since I had gone through some pretty horrific things in my childhood, I was entitled to do whatever I wanted, treat others like crap, and damn the repercussions. And getting shot was the Creator's way, I feel, of reintroducing me to humility.

The Creator must have been fed up with my ego and felt the divine need to teach me a lesson. I could just imagine him/her/it/both/all kicking it where holy beings kick it, plotting against me.

"Normally I get this shit out of the way at birth, so you won't grow to hate and scorn me, but take the lesson for what it is. You escaped that particular learning opportunity, so here is another one. I have to worry about wars and hunger and true evil, but your little cocky ass is getting just a bit too big for yourself. Didn't I give you enough pain to humble your ass? No? Well, here you go. Gunshot! Not so cocky now, are you?"

There is nothing that will humble your ass more than coming back from the dead with a hole in your stomach. Now let me break down how this newly acquired humility insinuated itself in my postmortem experience. Let's fast-forward a little.

I'm depressed and my gut throbs with a dull ache, but I am getting better. Well, aside from those kick-ass self-pity parties I would throw myself every second hour. I was just really getting into the groove of feeling sorry for myself when I heard a knock at the door. I asked who it was.

"It's Blue," came the muffled voice from the hallway.

I got up, let him in, and sat back down on the threadbare couch that had now become my bedroom, dining room, and therapist's chair.

"What up, B?" Blue said in his always happy, optimistic voice. You could detonate a bomb right next to him and he'd give you some positive words regarding how the bomb gave off both light *and* heat. "You are one bad motherfucker, surviving gunshots! Faster than a welfare check, more powerful than a pint of Ripple, able to leap turnstiles in a single bound. Look! In the NBA, in the NFL, it's Niggaman! What? They gonna make a comic book out of your ass."

He paused for a minute, looked around the apartment, eyes darting all over as if he were waiting for someone to drop in. What he said next made me sink lower than I already was.

"Yo, we got that dude for you, B."

"What do you mean, *got*?" I asked, reserving judgment until I had the answer.

Nervously smirking, Blue said, "Let's just say that it's gonna be hard for old boy to walk and talk."

"Y'all capped his ass?" Even as the question spilled from my lips, I really didn't want to know the answer.

Blue's matter-of-fact tone messed with me.

"Nah, we didn't shoot him. We thought about it, though. But if you take someone out, he's dead. He has no idea that he did anything wrong. But if you beat him down, beat his ass down real good, it serves as a constant reminder. Word life. You don't have to thank us, we're boys."

I guess that conversation was some type of catalyst because the very next day, I started to go through some changes. I began to understand some truths about myself. My situation could be looked at like a born-again scenario. I was reborn and had to realign myself with my new existence.

I took a deep breath and ventured outside for the first time since my death. Big-ass mistake. Not only did I have to realign myself but I also discovered that I was an enormous ball of fear. Well, I was only truly afraid of one thing, though: sudden noises that lasted for only a split second.

I'd be walking down the street and hear a car backfire, and it was all over for me. And it wasn't that zero-to-Mach-1 fear that gives you that extra boost of energy to either fight or escape. Oh no, that would have been too easy. The fear that struck me was that I-can't-move-and-I-don't-know-whether-I'm-going-to-shit-or-piss-myself absolute horror. I would just freeze up on any given sidewalk until some kindly person shook me from my paralysis, asking me if I were on drugs or just fucking stupid.

If the backfires were not enough, people popping their gum, utensils dropped on plates, hell, even a high-pitched sneeze would fossilize my ass. I told one of my kind-of friends about my noise phobia, and because of her big mouth, the entire neighborhood knew about it. Going to the store, I just knew that there were legions of little kids, running from tree to tree, whole rolls of bubble wrap tucked in their little bastard arms. I was their after-school program. Pop! Pop! Pop! To be frozen in midstride and hear an army of preteen giggles was pretty bad. But worse than this were the nightmares. The same two nightmares, over and over, night after night.

The first one was cinema vérité. It was hyperrealistic, reliving every moment of my shooting, informed of every minute detail. David Lynch directed the other dream, however, with Stephen King picking up scriptwriting chores. It went like this:

Me and my murderer—that's what he is, it doesn't mater that I came back—are in the same place where it all went down, but this time we're the only two people there. He slowly raises his gun, there is an enormous flash of light, and I see the bullet hurtling toward me. But the odd thing is, the bullet has a little face. It looks me in the eye and asks me, "Dick or the gut?"

"What?" I ask it.

"You heard me," it says. "Dick or the gut?"

There is really no need to contemplate the question any further. "Gut, please."

The bullet hits my stomach and begins to slowly burrow its way inside me, but there isn't any pain. I look down, and my stomach is becoming larger by the moment. The scene shifts, and I'm in stirrups and giving birth to a piece of bouncing-baby ammunition. I hop out of the stirrups and put the baby bullet in a stroller and then take it to the park so that it can play with all of the other baby bullets. My baby bullet calls me over to show me what it is playing with in one of those playground concrete tunnels. I crawl in and I see myself lying on my back, blood erupting from my belly button like a Las Vegas fountain. The baby bullet sticks its finger into my wound and giggles. That's some revolting shit.

But on this ride, the fun never stops. Those nightmares changed me.

Since I was arrogant, you'd think that I would use my coming back from the dead as a supreme bragging right. "Look! I came back from the dead. You can call me MC Rise Again."

But I'd been going through some sort of metamorphosis, and bragging about my situation seemed—anti-everything. Then paranoia set in. Why did I survive when a half dozen of my friends had been shot and hadn't come back? What was the catch? Did I come back for a reason? These questions—and their relatives—careened around my mind until I, in my infinite cockiness, figured that the Creator (whoever you envision it to be) had some "work" for me to do. At this moment, I swear that I heard a church bell. Maybe I heard it because I was standing across the street from St. Mark's, but still.

I'm fairly against modern interpretations of Christianity. I was back then, and I still am today. I'm not opposed to the idea of a God or Goddess or a Creative Ancestor, but organized religion causes so many problems. This isn't a theological debate, but it is, somewhat, a theological conversation.

The bell calls to me, and I decided—even though I'm not Catholic or even Christian—to speak to some ecclesiastical figure about my current circumstance. I wanted to know what the Creator had in store for me, and I felt that maybe one of the middlemen would have some answers. A bit of a warning: never, ever go looking for something to feed your spirit, or seek answers from the divine, when you look spiritually ravenous. There are folks out there who will twist your wants and needs every which way, using them as steps to their unscrupulous recruitment advantage, all in the name of what they perceive God/dess to be.

When I spoke with this particular priest, I felt like a seventeen-year-old girl getting off a Greyhound in pre-Giuliani Times Square. Those in the field of theology are the world's greatest seducers.

The priest glided down the hall and sat on the pew with almost no wasted motion. He extended a long, manicured hand and indicated that I should sit next to him. I sat, but I kept my distance. I looked around, and in the midst of the high ceilings, stained glass, candles, and stonework, I felt insignificant. This is another reason why I don't vibe with Christianity; everything about it (especially Catholicism) is designed to make you feel inferior. You should feel as if you are worshipping a divine entity out of a genuine expression of love and not because you are afraid to go to hell. And if I believed in hell, I'm sure that's where I would be heading for thinking that a man of the cloth was trying to pick up on me.

I told him my story in as much gory detail as I could, just to throw him off. Grossing out a priest would be a funny thing to tell all of my friends.

He nodded and listened to my tale, rubbed his hands together, and plied his trade.

"Christ is our savior, and all you have to do, to move past any difficulties, is trust in him. Really, he died for our sins. He was put up on a cross and crucified, but he came back. Just like you did." I would have sworn that his voice dropped and became more breathy the longer he spoke. "You believe that, don't you? That he died and came back? Just like you. You seem like a real smart young man, and I think you know that God has a plan for you, and I think you know what it is. If you didn't, you wouldn't have come here. God wants you to join our youth outreach network. They are all beautiful young, smart men such as yourself, and their mission in life is to spread God's word. You don't have to answer now, but I expect that I'll be seeing you around in the near future. I'll be waiting. God bless you."

Man, I couldn't get out of there fast enough. I felt unclean. That was one creepy experience, and it happened way before the deluge of priest molestation scandals. That interaction turned me even farther away from any form of Christianity, but I still had the strange idea that some sort of religious instruction was needed. Being twice as determined to find *the answer*, I decided that I should go to a synagogue. Really.

Saying too much about this will come really close to delving into stereotypes, but I'm a big fan of full disclosure. Mind you, I was wholly ignorant of the rules and rituals and everything else associated with Jewish religious life. I just felt a kinship based on our people's getting treated like shit for thousands of years.

Putting on my best suit, I strolled to the synagogue. *Guess Who's Coming to Temple?* I didn't even make it past the front steps. Aside from a later encounter with some Nazi skinheads, I never felt so much hatred directed toward me. From the elders to the kids, I was looked at as if I was moonwalking, butt naked, sodomizing a pig while eating shellfish. I tried adopting a nonaggressive stance—a social adaptation that all black men master when in the presence of perceived white people—to show that I had come to parlay, not disrupt. This one old, wrinkled walnut of a man said, "I don't know why he's here. Maybe he's Sammy Davis the third." Even I had to laugh. It wasn't ha-ha funny but damn-that-old-bastard-got-me-good funny. The score now stood: religion two, Shawn zero. What the hell, I thought. I might as well go for the Abrahamic hat trick. Next stop, Muslims and the mosque.

Let me stop lying. I went and spoke to a Black Muslim on the street corner. Those cats always impressed me.

Almost all of them had a level of charisma that coerced you into listening to what they had to say. They dressed sharp, seemed to be unafraid of anything, spoke with a fountain of energy, and knew obscure yet fascinating facts such as how much the earth weighed. When I approached, I was bombarded by the rhetoric.

"*Final Call! Final Call!* I got that good news for ya. Brother! Black man! What can I do for you today? Bean pie? Don't live to eat, eat to live. Do you want a paper? Pie? Paper? Paper? Pie?" I told him my story and explained that I was looking for what could only be called enlightenment.

"Enlightenment? Illumination? To make the dark bright? That sounds like a colonized mind at work. Why is the darkness so bad, brother? Blackness is demonized all day, every day, and to witness a brother buy into the white man's lies hurts." I explained that I wanted to know what the Creator wanted from me.

"That's a tall order, brother, but by the grace of Allah, I think that I can help you out. The white man, as you most assuredly know, is the true and honest personification of evil. From the Tuskegee experiment to the transatlantic slave trade to having our people believe that milk is actually good for them, they have proven that they only harbor negative intentions for our people. And it is the duty of Allah's chosen people to bring this message to the masses."

I absorbed what he said, and then I countered, "Yo, that's all well and good. But it was a brother that shot me in the stomach and took my life."

My bow-tied homeboy stayed on message. "But I bet you it was a white man who made the gun."

We were now moving into my pet peeve territory— adhering to a party line just because it is *the* party line within your specific ideology. I'm not a big fan of the sheep people, especially in religion and politics, but I'm not one to walk away from an argument.

"You may be right," I halfway conceded. "But no white man made that brother carry the gun around, single me out, and pull that trigger." He must have been new because my words seemed to overload his circuits.

"Are you sure that you don't want some pie, my brother? You don't want a paper, do you? Some pie? A paper? A'Salaam Alaikum." His avoidance of the argument pissed me off.

"Salami and bacon. Bye, conspiracy theory man. Good-bye."

Needless to say, I was getting nowhere. I was frustrated to the point that I wanted to give up and return to my life as a TV-watching, couch-lounging member of the legion of the depressed. I sought divine answers from three disparate sources, and they had all let me down. What was that all about? It wasn't fair. Why wasn't I allowed to have what so many others have—a relationship with something bigger than myself? As I was voluntarily sinking into despair, it hit me: Buddhism. But before that, I want to address something that my editor asked me as he was going through the book. He wanted to know why I hadn't sought out African spirituality or African American churches, such as the AME Church, for example. It's a fair question.

I didn't bother looking for any African faith system because my interactions with Africans in America had all been negative. The prejudice that many Africans harbor toward American-born blacks is more intense than that of some whites. One African dude told me that African Americans squandered their freedom. Instead of taking advantage of the university and other opportunities, they spent more time and money on their clothes and cars than on purchasing houses or opening stores in their own neighbors. Ouch. When he said this, I was ready to fight him. But looking back, it makes me sick to say that I kind of agree with him.

As for the black church, it seems so damn anachronistic. A pre–civil rights holdover. An institution more concerned with profits than prophets. There was just something so backward, so country about the black church. I was a modern man, and big hats, fans, and singing old-school Negro spirituals put me way too close to slavery. I wasn't feeling any parts of it. I know that the black church has done a lot of good for a lot of people, but it wasn't hip enough for me. Told you I was arrogant.

But Buddhism was something that I thought I could get with. It was a perfect belief system for where I was at the time: compassion, elimination of the ego, this existence is mere illusion, and the way to enlightenment is to rid one's self of illusions. That shit made sense. No genuflecting and creepy attempted pickups, no feeling like an unwanted outsider, no selling pies or papers. I could get with this. I was about to meet the cosmos face-to-face. There wouldn't be any middlemen, just my mission to destroy the illusions that I clung to. I was down.

When I hit the Buddhist spot, the first thing that popped out was that none of the one-hundred-plus people looked anything like me. I hung in the cuts, observing, for the first few times I attended the service, and the colorscape never changed. During one of the services, I must have been visibly distressed, because this *Buffy the Vampire Slayer*–looking girl flitted up to me, a half-moon smile creasing her face. The scary thing was I truly believe that old girl read my mind.

"Like, don't worry, brother. We are all just, like, one big, blessed ball of Buddha consciousness. Color is, like, so irrelevant."

It would have been so cool to be able to take her at her word, but then I noticed that there weren't any Asians represented. Not even a Hapa. I'm thinking to myself, how can this be an Asian belief system and there aren't any Asians here?

You can call me prejudiced if you want, but there is this little thing that I dig on called authenticity.

If I want to listen to the Isley Brothers, I'm going to listen to the Isley Brothers, not punk-ass Michael Bolton. If I want some Caribbean food, I'm going to either cook it or get it from a Caribbean restaurant—I will not be eating at some fucked-up California *fusion* joint. And if I was going to participate in a serious study of Buddhism, I would want to get my lessons from someone who has some cultural lineage to the system. If I don't get it from as close to the source as possible, the shit is not real to me.

Needless to say my Buddhist days did not last too long. But the ideas behind the faith had me gassed. Investigating the faith further, I finally got my mind around a number of the more basic tenets. I eventually sorted out some of what I was absorbing.

Shit hit me like a rock. The Four Noble Truths are very powerful, and I feel that they are especially appropriate for black men going through an existential crisis. What follows is my interpretation of them:

The entire world is suffering.

This suffering is our fault because we cling to things.

It is possible to eliminate this suffering.

We eliminate this suffering through Buddhist practice.

This works for me, but the above is taken out of Buddhist context. I don't believe in karma (although I do believe that we pay for our negative behavior because we slip up and get caught or exposed), and this is another reason why I couldn't adhere to Buddhism. In my limited understanding, karma is akin to a weight hanging around a person's neck that gets heavier and heavier with every incarnation of said person's life. This idea did not work for my situation. First, the idea of an individual living multiple lives? I just can't get my head around it. But if it is true, what the hell did I do in my past lives to deserve being shot and killed, being brought back to life, then experiencing a spiritual and nervous breakdown? I really did not want to know who that person was. This paradigm did not jibe with what I considered reality, so I had to move on. But I had no real idea where.

After all of this religious exploration, I still felt hollow. What, if anything, was I supposed to do with my new life? Should I just consider my rebirth a blind and lucky accident and move on? Or was there something that I was destined to do? I know it looks as if I was engaged in an exercise of the ego, but I was pretty freaked out.

My whole life had been linked to violence.

Whether it was done to me or I was doing it to someone else, violence had been an integral part of my history, and up until getting shot I figured that violence was just people hurting one another, a natural and accepted way to solve problems. It was easy to justify with buzzwords and pat phrases: "poverty," "wrong place, wrong time," "That's what ghetto kids do," "I'm a dude, what do you expect?" "He shouldn't have looked at me that way."

But being shot was different.

I was forced to take a look at all of the violent instances in my life and see them as more than just random occurrences. And you'd think that this would be liberating, but it wasn't. Instead of finding hidden truth within these violent acts, I just became more critical of myself. Maybe *critical* isn't the word; *hyper-self-pitying* is more accurate. Have you ever had one of those I'm-being-an-asshole moments?

All of this cerebral, emotional, metaphysical exploration was not who I was. I acted. I lived so much more in my body than in my head. Truth be told, I was surprised that I had the capacity to think along these lines—a Creator, causality, and faith—but I was a somatic type of cat, and in all of my explorations, I had completely abandoned my body. I don't know if it was because of the damage it had sustained, but I felt I had to reengage my physical self. And—as banal as it seems—just like that, I decided to go dancing. Dancing started all of this, and I hoped it would give me some sort of answer.

I am aware that this is going into New Age territory, but bear with me.

Back in the day—when men could dance without their sexual orientation being questioned—going to the club on the sixteen-to-twenty nights was like a homecoming. I knew everyone from the doorman to the waitstaff to most of the club goers, and they all knew me—it was my ghetto Cheers. And we all used to dance—b-boying. But when b-boying lost its luster, I become a head bobber, dancing with just my neck and head. There was something about abandoning oneself to the music, pushing one's body to the limit, taking physical risks that did not involve violence. Dancing represented a time when I could allow myself to feel vulnerable. I miss that.

While walking to the club, my stomach began to knot. This was the first time I'd been out in my greater social sphere since the shooting, and I had no idea how people were going to react. Hell, I didn't know if any of the people I knew would still be there. The whole nightlife business is a fluid one, and things change without any type of warning.

I bypassed the snaking line and stepped right up to Big John. He hated the term *bouncer* and preferred either *doorman* or *gatekeeper*. He'd much rather use his mouth than his fists, but with ebony Volkswagens for biceps, he rarely had to raise his voice above a whisper to calm rowdy patrons. Big John glanced at me, and we instantly fell into our game.

This game had continued for as long as I'd been going to the club, and I can't tell you how we started it. It was our intellectual, alpha-male pissing contest. He respected me for my combination of brains, fighting talent, and size, and I respected him for the same things—and we both believed that we knew everything about black culture.

In the hood, it was rare for a brother to openly and proudly proclaim his intelligence. It took me a while to do so, but by following Big John's lead, I grew to accept my position as a hip bookworm with violent tendencies and zero luck with women. You have to be comfortable with where you are.

We quizzed each other about black history, art, and science, and then I stumped him. I asked, "Who is the most prominent black male heterosexual science fiction writer?" By this time, a crowd had swarmed around us, waiting for an answer. Watching a person think is some funny shit, especially if the person is as expressive as Big John. His face looked like chocolate taffy, pulling and stretching, not willing to settle on a shape until he had found the correct answer.

I patted him on the shoulder and said, "Steven Barnes." Big John rolled his eyes and laughed a multidecibel laugh. "You lent me that cat's book, *Streetlethal*. Damn. Get your ass inside." As I brushed past him, he put his dinner plate–sized hand on my shoulder and looked me in the eye—something that was just not done on the streets, no matter how friendly you were—and told me that he was glad to see me and that he was happy I was up and around. I gave him the hetero-handshake-and-hug combination and entered the club.

Once you pass the threshold of a nightclub, you enter a completely different world. It is actually quite mythic. Everyone (including you) is wearing a mask of some kind. And your true face is revealed only in the darkness between bursts of strobe light. You catch glimpses of angels and demons, predators and prey, every time the light disappears.

The dance floor was this living, seething, undulating entity that I wanted nothing more than to be a part of. Tiptoeing my way to the edge, I felt this little tangle of fear in my belly, and my wound started aching. Phantom pain, to be sure, but it still stopped me from taking any further steps. Gulping air, I gave myself over to the lights, the music, the movement. Walking a couple of paces, I hit the dance floor and was immediately comfortable. I moved a bit and could not believe how stiff I was—and kind of angry that I wasn't able to dance the way I used to. I hoped that it would get better in time. The longer I danced, more and more moves opened themselves up to me, and I really started to enjoy myself.

That is, until I was bumped by Brothersaurus Rex.

I moved away from him, but he, somehow, was in my space and bumped me again. If he knew how to dance, it wouldn't have been so bad, but he danced like chickens fuck, so his actions were unforgivable. He bumped me a third time, and I gave a little back to him. I can tolerate most things, but I firmly believe that assholes should know they're being assholes. You make a mistake or do something stupid, I'm going to let you know. And I expect you to do the same.

After bumping Brothersaurus, I felt my violent energy begin to rise, and I knew it was time for me to exit the dance floor and go calm down somewhere. B.S. (before shooting), I would have snapped on the dude and launched a punch to his face. But now, my relationship with unnecessary violence was changing. And, to be truthful, I didn't want to get popped in the gut and find out that whatever the doctors did wasn't enough to hold everything in place. See, I knew that this cat was trying to pull me into a confrontation, but I wasn't having it, so I turned to leave.

His six-pound hand landed on my shoulder, spinning me around to face him. I thought to myself, I've been here before, recently. And the last time, I died. I am not going through that shit again. Who knows if I'd come back? More than likely, this one, this death, would stick. Death was holding my rain check, ready to redeem it, and I was not about to let him.

Brothersaurus drew his fist back, but don't think for a moment I was just going to let him sock me. I may have been on the path to a less violent lifestyle, but I was not going out like that. I put my dukes up, ready to scrap. While all of this was jumping off, I was wondering how in the hell I wound up here again. Are black men that fucked up? I braced myself and got ready to exchange blows.

But before the fight even happened, Big John, like some dark chocolate superhero, swooped in, in rolling blackout style, and mashed Brothersaurus Rex. Just imagine if Mount Kilimanjaro had arms, legs, a fade haircut, a pager, and a pair of Adidas Superstars. The scuffle lasted no more than a few seconds, and Brothersaurus was shown the door. I may have been trying to live a more peaceful life, but I could still admire an expert ass whooping. Damn.

Big John came back and was really sincere. "You've been through enough already. Enjoy the rest of the night and don't let this shit get you down. You in my house; ain't nothing going to happen to you." He hugged me and went about his duties.

It tripped me out to realize how men are willing to involve themselves in their friends' beefs but won't let you borrow five dollars. They'll take a beating for you but will rarely, if ever, give you any money. I know this is an awkward aside, but it is something that still makes me think. It seems as if black men have adopted the American view of their bodies: big black tools that are low on the priority list and deserved to be damaged.

Foolishly, I thought that I had come full circle and survived the experience. Dancing to violence, to death, to rebirth, to dancing, to violence, to life. And in this second violent encounter, I hadn't even had to throw a punch. Full circle, my ass. I'd only come about halfway.

Looking around, I knew I couldn't stay in the club, despite Big John's oath to protect me. This whole scene was now a footnote in the new life I was trying to build for myself. I tossed off a good-bye and left.

As I was walking to the train station, I felt something missing. Fear. I had almost gotten into a serious brawl, and even though trace amounts of adrenaline pumped through my system, there was no fear in my body. You have to understand—this was the first time that I had been fear-free since I had been shot. It was exhilarating, but I have no idea why my fear decided to leave at that moment. The only thing I can think of is that I had survived a violent encounter. Hell, I didn't even have to engage in the violent encounter. But my survival had nothing to do with me or my actions. My survival was purely happenstance. Shit, you take what you can get and call it a success.

My walk had a little more spring to it, and I felt myself smiling. It was kind of like that movie *Singin' in the Rain*, when Gene Kelly is jumping around, dancing, because at that particular moment in time, life was just so damn wonderful. That is exactly how I felt, but instead of Arthur Freed writing the lyrics to the song I was singing, Main Source handled those chores quite nicely.

This elation came out of nowhere. Maybe it was due to some self-realization or some type of subconscious defense mechanism for male stupidity, but clarity is some shit. The Buddhist folks hit the nail on the head: The world is an illusion created by our egos and context, and once you get rid of it all, the simple truth is that even though life is the most beautiful thing there is, it is what it is—just a life. No better or worse than any other. It is something to embrace but not hold on to so tightly that you are worse for the embrace. I had wasted so much time being afraid, hiding from my life, feeling sorry for myself that—hell, let me get real—this was the first time I had ever thought that life was beautiful, and like a crack fiend, I've been chasing that feeling ever since. And in the pursuit of this feeling, I had a rudimentary, albeit pretty dangerous, idea of what I was supposed to do.

Fancying myself a detective, I spent the better part of the following day tracking down where the dude who shot me lived. I won't give his real name, but we'll call him "Jerry." Dude lived around the corner from me. I hate to say it, but this is how it is in the projects. The people who deal you the most damage are those in closest proximity. It's not like there is a rival gang coming across town to mess with you—it is a rival gang that lives across the street, down the block, or, in a bit of personal history, in the same projects but across the common area.

It was something straight out of a cowboy flick. Walking toward his building, everyone stopped to look at me, assembling a threat analysis. Kids stopping playing, clockers stopped dealing, and, I swear, even the rats stopped scavenging in order to figure out who I was and what the hell I was doing there. They knew I didn't belong there, I knew that I didn't belong there, and the whole thing could go ass-end up in a second. If, even for a moment, the people around there thought that I was a problem—or worse, a snitch—I'd never make it to the front doors of Jerry's building.

Holding my breath, I eased on by the group of toughs who were milling about the ground floor. The heat of their scrutiny bathed me, and I began to feel a bit claustrophobic. Imperceptibly, a pair of the hard asses moved, clearing my path to the stairs. Ten flights of stairs later, I was on the fifth floor, in front of apartment 572.

Motivations are the worst, especially when you don't know, fully, what is driving them. Here I was, just outside the enemy's camp and rolling solo. I had not one idea what was waiting for me on the other side of the door. But I'm stand-ing there, trying to stare through the peephole and hoping I have made the correct decision by showing up. Without con-scious volition, I knocked on the door.

I knocked again. The faint light that was spilling from the peephole went dark; someone was looking at me. Bracing myself for the omnipresent, ghetto-gruff voice asking, "Who is it?" and not knowing what to say, I was surprised when I heard all seven locks being clicked.

The flimsy wooden door eased open, and there was this tiny old woman staring up at me. We looked at each other for a moment and looked at each other some more. What the hell was I supposed to say? "Someone in this house shot and killed me, and I would like to speak with him?" That would work.

Her face was so calm, but with just a hint of "you better not do shit" under the surface. I could tell she knew that something was wrong but wasn't exactly sure what it was. It was the old woman who broke the conversational stalemate. "What do you want, boy?"

"I'm here to see Jerry, ma'am," I said, as politely as I could. "Is he home?"

"Yes," she said.

"Can I speak with him, please?" I put all of my black Eddie Haskell charm in the asking.

Shrugging, she turned her back to me, opened the door wider, and walked inside. I followed her in, making sure to leave the door open, just in case I had to get out of there in a hurry. Normally, I have a fair number of hand skills and can hold my own in any physical confrontation, but being shot kind of killed my confidence, and I wasn't so sure that, if it came down to it, I'd be able to scrap like I used to. So I had to keep the lines of retreat clear and available.

The apartment was ghetto immaculate. It was that type of clean that only older, poor people could accomplish. Incense was burning, the plastic on the couch and love seat was taut and shiny, and there was not a speck of dust anywhere. Just because you're broke doesn't mean you have to be trashy.

Moving deeper into the apartment, I saw him. He was sitting on the floor, eating a bowl of cereal, watching *Danger Mouse*. The old woman—whom I assume was Jerry's grandmother—kept hawkeyed vigil from the kitchenette, her hand absently caressing a black iron frying pan.

There he was, my killer.

Creeping closer, I could see some scars on his face, bald head, and arms. My boys did some work on him. It must have been fifteen seconds until he looked up, and a wave of anger and nausea filled me. Just by the way he glanced at me, I could tell he had no idea who I was.

"Who are you?" Jerry asked, standing, cereal bowl still in his hand.

I slid into my defensive stance and asked Jerry to sit down. When he didn't budge, I put a little bit of that street in my voice and told him to do what I had asked him a second ago. Shockingly, he sat down. Well, at least I still had it.

I pulled up a wooden dining room chair and set it down with enough space between us so that I couldn't reach him and he couldn't reach me without some sort of effort.

Leaning in, I told him my full name. If he didn't recognize my face, he damn sure wouldn't recognize my name, but I felt that it was important for him to know who I was.

I then got what my friend Warnell calls the "Ghost." It's when your words are controlled by something other than your conscious thoughts. Warnell is a Baptist minister, and he attributes it to God. I'm attributing my Ghost experience to fear, stupidity, sadness, and a desire to move past my fear and pain.

"You don't recognize me, do you?" I lifted my shirt and showed him the bullet wound that had taken the place of my navel.

"Does this look familiar? It should, because you did this to me. You shot me over some bullshit. Over dancing! Now you recognize me, don't you? I won't lie—I'm thinking about killing your ass right now, but I won't. Not because my people already got to your ass, and not because I'm on your block, and not even because that old lady is holding a frying pan. None of that shit matters. The only reason that your ass ain't dead already is because . . . I could have stepped up in here with mad crew, or worse, I could have came in here with five-oh and had your punk ass thrown in jail, but I didn't. It's just you and me."

The Ghost was on a roll.

"It's just you and me. I wanted you to see my face, in the light, and I wanted to see what is left of yours. B, you shot me. You killed me. You took my life! You stole two and a half minutes from me, but I came back. I didn't come back for revenge, B; I came back to live. That's all. That's it. Nothing bigger or smaller than that. I came back to live my life. You know what I'm going to do with this life? I'm going to forgive you. This ain't no type of God shit; I'm forgiving you because you need it, and every time you look at your Frankenstein face, you'll know that it could have been a whole lot worse. So, I forgive you for killing me."

The Ghost left, and I could have easily fallen asleep in that apartment, but it wouldn't have been the best of ideas. Body shaking, sweat pouring out of everywhere, I got up and left the scene of the craziest thing I have ever done. I said goodbye to the old woman and headed home.

It's funny, but when I speak at high schools and civic groups and tell this story, it is hard for many people to believe. They think that I'm embellishing it or outright lying or that no one would be stupid enough to forgive someone who shot them. The most bizarre accusation is that I am pretending to be a good guy, and I really sneaked back and killed Jerry. None of this is even remotely accurate.

I did what I did for me. It was a purely selfish act. I was becoming a new person, just coming into my own version of a positive self, and that was my first act within that new life. My actions allowed me to get out of the projects and pursue dreams that would have been killed if I had stayed in the projects and clung to my project mentality.

In a way, I'm kind of thankful for being shot and coming back. If it hadn't happened, I assure you that I would be selling dope, boosting cars, in jail, or dead. I can't believe I just wrote that I was thankful for being shot. Nothing will humble your ass more than coming back from the dead. Trust me, I know.

Was Jerry ever incarcerated for his crime? No, he wasn't. We didn't turn to the cops for help—not that they'd be willing to help us anyway. We handled our own business. You mess with us, and we'd mess right back, damn the consequences. Our neighborhood was *our* neighborhood and we did what we had to do to take care of our own. But there is more to it than just this.

Telling on him would have belittled the experience. If I reported it, my shooting would have been just another crime and not the transformative experience that it turned into. But by forgiving him, and letting him know that I knew he blasted me—there's something to that. I now have some dirt on Jerry. I have some power over this dude. It sounds creepy, to be sure, but I thoroughly enjoy knowing that I can pop into his life, at any time, and force him to face his misdeeds. I haven't seen him since our last encounter, but I might feel the urge to do so and I don't want the guy to be in jail. I enjoy thinking about him questioning every nanosecond of the freedom he currently enjoys.

I said that I forgave him, and I did. But I didn't say that I forgot. And I won't.

Hair, Hugs, and Drums

After recovering—physically, mentally, and emotionally—
from being shot, I reinvested in my life and my pursuit of a
progressive black masculinity. Most of my interactions with
men had either a competitive or violent tinge, and I wanted
something more. I had male friends, but they were just as confused as I was, so we really couldn't learn from one another.
All we could do was pass misinformation back and forth like
an ill-formed ping-pong ball. I wanted some sort of mentor,
a guide through all of the crap. An older guy—someone who
had already been through it, who had it together and was willing to share it with me in a way that wasn't just pure theory,
who had actual tools to help me on my journey.

Thinking back, I have no idea why I was so determined
to become "a good man." My grandfather was a good man,
but the poor old guy seemed archaic. Granddad was a
Depression-era relic, all suits and hats, hopelessly out of touch
with the now and the just-a-little-bit-after-now. He was who
I wanted to be when I became a senior citizen; there was no
way I could be like him in my current state. He was my in-

the-distant-future self, but I needed a template for my present self.

On the other hand, my uncle, Granddad's son, was cooler than anything. He had the right clothes, right car, and right language; he could dance his ass off, and all the girls loved him. But there was something missing when I looked in his eyes. He was putting up a front. With every half smile and overenthusiastic greeting, he was hiding something. I don't really want to put his business out there, but according to the whisper stream, my beloved uncle was involved in some very high-level, less-than-legal enterprises. I was on a completely different path than he was, so I had to find my own way. And this way, according to my weird little code, had to be genuine. Even though I was dishonest with people around 70 percent of the time, I wanted to be honest and genuine with myself.

I wanted to be someone completely different from the limited repository of masculinity that had affected my life. I was going to be that one dude who got out of the projects, didn't cheat on his girlfriend, had the respect and love of other men—not their respect based on fear—and was just an all-around cool dude. But first, I needed to figure out how to get over the overwhelming anxiety my personal masculinity caused.

There are very few avenues of instruction relating to masculinity and there is almost nothing about black masculinity. In recent years, you have a few brothers—Kevin Powell, Michael Datcher, Scott Poulson-Bryant, Nathan McCall—tackling these issues in a public way, but back then it was a white dude's sandbox. Hence my reading of Robert Bly's *Iron John: A Book About Men*, from which I emerged more confused and angry than I had been before I started. No quest for masculine information can be undertaken without having to contend with *Iron John*.

To put it bluntly, that book does way too much. Overinterpretation is much too kind a description. I'll give Bly credit for attacking the subject with such fire in his belly, but it was one of the whitest books I have ever read. There was no entry point for me. All of these Russo-European folktales had nothing to do with me at the time. If I read the book now, I could do some comparative research and find African and Caribbean folktales and myths that would give me the same lessons. The book made me feel excluded from the masculine experience.

When *Iron John* first dropped, it was kind of the vanguard of the early 1990s men's movement. Just what this movement entailed is still debatable—as well as what, if anything, it accomplished. But one of the good things it did was to put the exploration of masculinity into the public consciousness.

One day I was reading the book in this cafe around the corner from my house—it was sort of the intellectual, transcultural hub of the neighborhood. This means that all types of folks went there to hang about, explore the Big Questions, and prey on people they thought were intellectually or philosophically inferior. The place was a social stage where folks performed projections of their highest aspirations.

I'm reading the book, highlighting passages and jotting angry notes in the margins, when this younger version of Tolkien's Gandalf sat down uninvited. I pretended not to notice him, but he had this creepy energy. Making a big show about putting the book away, I met Gandalf's eyes and put some bass in my voice, "What do you want, B?"

Indicating the book, Gandalf tilted his hat back and broke into a huge smile, "That book, right there, is the truth." He nodded as if his pronouncement should be taken so as well.

"It's a'ight," I shot back, putting a little bit of that black male swagger in my voice and shoulders, not too much but just enough to scare average white folks. Obviously, old boy wasn't average.

"That book is the bible, an instruction manual, for a new consciousness. It lays manhood bare and shows us how to deal with our masculine powers." He had the look of a religious convert, all glassy eyed and eager drooling. He leaned in. The closer he got, the more he looked like that wizened fictional sorcerer. "But the bible is just words on a page until you put them into practice."

OK, now I was intrigued. "What do you mean, 'practice'?"

He held out his hand. "I'm Alexander." Shaking his hand, I told him my name. I was under his spell. Alexander then launched into one of the world's greatest sales pitches for the burgeoning men's movement. The way he presented the practice, it seemed as if he were speaking about a superhero training ground. Groups of men were meeting in the forests of the world, getting in touch with their primal energies, banging on drums to conjure ancestral male spirits, and jumping in, on, around, and through fire. This ghetto kid was at once fascinated (wow! mentors!) and repelled (white people do some crazy shit!) by the thought of joining one of these groups. But by the end of his spiel, I was down.

Alexander gave me his number and told me there was a retreat that weekend, and he would love for me to attend. It was upstate, and he had no problem driving me there and back home. I gave him my address and thanked him for inviting me. When he left, I sort of came to my senses and asked aloud, "What the hell did I get myself into?"

The wait was excruciating. I was—and still am—something of a control freak, so not knowing what was about to happen made for a restless couple of days. My mind wandered, and I created all sorts of crazy situations, most definitely letting my imagination get the best of me. But the imagined situation that continually asserted itself was that I'd be taken upstate and brought to a KKK meeting. I'd be given a five-minute head start; then the Klan, along with an army of dogs, would chase me down, and when they finally caught me I'd be lynched from a tall tree and the dogs would tear at my bare feet. The sad part was that I didn't think that my being tricked into becoming the festivities at a Klan meeting was too far-fetched. Also, this man training was being conducted in the woods, the undisputed home of psycho white boys. See the film *Deliverance* for more details.

I am, and always will be, a product of the urban environment. I'm a concrete, steel, and glass type of guy, and I don't understand *nature*. I appreciate it for the oxygen, food, medicines, and beauty it provides, but I cannot be in it for more than a few hours. I tried camping once, and it was one of the most stressful things that I had ever done. Things were scurrying underneath, trees were creaking, and when it got dark I thought I'd lose my mind. I'm so used to the light-bleed of cities; I find it comfortable.

When I'm walking at night, the ambient illumination makes me feel secure. I don't feel so alone. But when I was camping, seeing the sky for what it truly is, a vast foreverness, I felt as if I did not matter; I was just this insignificant, Negroidal speck of a nonfactor. And being as self-centered as I sometimes can be, I wasn't feeling that. Also, there are animals out there, and I don't do too well with animals. Anything that is stronger than me, with teeth and claws, I don't fool with. They stay out of my home, and I'll stay out of theirs.

Saturday arrived, and I still had a few reservations about this whole trip. I didn't know where I was going, I had no idea who Alexander was, and I had to go to the damn woods. I could be killed up there, and no one would have any idea. The intercom buzzed, signaling the moment of truth. Fuck it, I thought to myself. I could fight, I could run, and if worse comes to worst, I could steal his car and get back home. Stealing a car was not anything out of the ordinary for me. I picked up my bag, pocketed a knife, and went downstairs.

All of the neighborhood's eyes were on Alexander and his Toyota Supra. The car looked like something out of science fiction. It was silver and sleek and emanated speed. Much to my surprise, Alexander was twelve feet from the car and the engine was running. Twelve feet? That was a mile to an experienced car thief. Scanning the faces of my people, I could tell that a few of them were thinking along the same lines. I gave them a look, hopefully indicating that I had my own plans for the dude and his car. A couple of the jackers backed off. Respect and honor among low-level thieves is not a cliché nor is it overrated. With the eyes of an entire project block staring, I got into the Supra and we took off.

I had never been in anything so plush. The seats were leather, Alexander had a mobile phone—even though it was the size of a tin of pound cake, back then it was incredible—and he drove the car with the skill and confidence of the best car thieves. His weaving in and out of traffic was almost hypnotic, and I felt myself starting to drift off. Alexander must have noticed. "You can sleep if you want to. We have about another hour or so." His voice snapped me back to full attention. I bet that is exactly what he wanted. To have a black man asleep and at his mercy would be a feather in his Klan cap. I bit the shit out of the inside of my lip, the pain making me alert and just a bit ornery.

One minute we were on the highway, and the next, with just a slight turn of the steering wheel, Alexander brought us into some Lord of the Rings–looking glade. Straight. Up. Woods. The trees and the grass were an unimaginable green; the sun that seeped through the treetops was a deep yellow gold, and the smell was so crisp that I felt as if I were in a salad. Needless to say, I was in awe, humbled, and scared as hell, all at the same time. Strangely, it was a good feeling.

I was more than happy to see we were parked right off the park's entrance. If it came down to it, I could boost the car and hit the road with quickness.

We exited the car and made our way to the campsite. Suddenly the full weight of my culture shock came crashing down so hard that I almost stumbled. The woods were quiet, but it was an alien quiet. Even though there were birds singing, it didn't matter. The silence was almost like an entity. A foreboding entity was telling my ass to get out of there as soon as possible, and I was really about to listen. But I trooped on to where the rest of the men were creating a mini man-city. Barbecues were set up every dozen feet, tents were all over the place, and dudes were playing the drums, tossing around baseballs and footballs, and droning on the didgeridoo. It was like some kind of tweaked, testosterone-imbued Renaissance fair.

As soon as Alexander and I came closer, a pair of shirtless guys approached to help us with our stuff.

"This is the guy you were telling us about?" said one of the guys, who looked like a cross between Ralph Kramden, of *Honeymooners* fame, and G. Gordon Liddy.

Alexander nodded.

"Welcome home," said the other, vaguely ethnic-looking guy. "You're in for a life-changing experience."

They led us over to where we were to pitch our tent and left us to it. I asked Alexander why the guys didn't stay to help us set up.

"Because each man has to do for himself. They set their camp, and we have to set ours," came his reply.

Truth be told, I didn't lend one finger to the whole setting-up-camp thing. I watched as Alexander expertly assembled the tent, dug a fire pit, and then, in a move that almost caused me to heave, yanked his shirt off. He was in pretty good shape for an old dude, but his chest was covered with a frosty white pelt with little liver spots peeking through. I do have to admit that I was a bit jealous of how comfortable he and the other men were with walking around bare chested, but it seemed a bit too gay for my taste, so my shirt stayed on.

A horn sounded. Not a sax or a trumpet or any other piece of brass, but an actual horn. Some dude who looked just like Marvel Comics' Thor was actually blowing into something that had once belonged to an animal. There he was, the Norse god of thunder, standing on a rock, chest and stomach almost overly defined, long blond hair trailing down his back, head tossed back, pushing air through some sort of pearlescent antler. I was in the hood no longer.

The bellow of the horn was the call for everyone to gather around. Silently, we all made a semicircle around the horn blower and waited for his words. Out of all the men assembled, I was the only one not waiting for the dude to speak. All of their eyes were transfixed on Thor on his rocky pedestal, and it kind of creeped me out. I'm not one to show blind allegiance to anyone, not even my friends or family. I question everything, but these men seemed to be paying almost fanatical attention to Thor. Not one person, aside from myself, was even moving.

He spoke with an almost imperceptible accent. I had no idea where he was from, but he used his voice like an instrument, ebbing to a lull and then rising to a crescendo, moving from a whisper to a volcanic eruption. I wasn't paying too much attention to what he was saying, but I did find myself cheering with the rest of the men when he finished.

Charged with some sort of fire, the crowd changed locations from the foot of the rock to a slightly muddy clearing. Now everyone had his shirt off and was limbering up. Men were stretching, doing push-ups and sit-ups, loosening their limbs, looking as if they were ready to fight. And this is exactly what they were about to do. This I could get with.

Alexander popped up next to me and explained that we were about to engage in a "one-fall" wrestling match. This meant that all you had to do was throw a guy down on his back to win. He then told me that I didn't have to participate. I smiled at him and took off my shirt.

The rules were quite simple. Two men enter the circle, and the winner stays there until he is slammed on his back. Some men were winners for just a couple of seconds, while others had to go through five or six other dudes until they were deposed. There wasn't any type of order. If you felt it, you jumped in to either whoop or get whooped.

I felt that male energy rise, that energy that causes you to believe that you are way stronger and faster than you actually are. I knew that I was tough, but I damn sure wasn't as tough as I was pumping myself up to be. Just before I got into the circle, I looked around and noticed that there was not one other person darker than I was and that the closest complexion to mine was three to four shades lighter, and he was Asian. I could get my ass beat and not have one ounce of backup. Fuck it, I thought. If I'ma go out, I'ma go out swinging.

Soon as I stepped into the circle, I heard the chant of "new guy." I was two ways about this. Being the new guy meant either they were going to take it easy on me or they were going to try to beat my ass.

Alexander appeared right in the inside edge of the circle and shot me a thumbs-up. What was this, an eighties action movie? I gave him that ghetto nod and held my arms out, daring anyone to step up. A feral-looking dude about my age decided to come get some.

With his near-white hair tied up in a ponytail, dude stalked to about three feet from me. Unlike the other matches, mine did not start right away. There was a tension between us that stopped us from rushing at each other. We circled, sized each other up, and with a low growl, Ponytail tried to tackle me at the legs. Sidestepping, I spun and made a grab for his shoulders but was about an inch too short. I could see him working himself up. He had a mad on for me, and I had no idea why. Most of the other matches seemed friendly, but there was no friendship or fraternity in what was going down between the two of us. We could take it there if he wanted to. Wheeling around, he came at me full speed.

No matter how fast you are, you are not that fast moving backward. And there is no way that you can move faster backward than someone can moving forward, so I was screwed. Ponytail crashed into me, and I almost fell flat on my back. We locked arms and tried our damnedest to slam one another to the dirt. We must have been clenched for a half minute, and I knew that I was going to catch a bad one in just a few more seconds.

That is, unless I cheated.

Faking a sneeze, I shot a wad of snot and saliva right in Ponytail's face. It was so nasty I was almost ashamed of myself. Almost.

Feeling him falter, I shoved my hip into Ponytail's side and judo-flipped him on his back. The roar of the crowd was deafening. I was on some warrior shit. I raised my arms above my head and let out the most cavemanesque yell possible. Never did that before, but it felt good.

I looked down at Ponytail and wondered why he didn't get up immediately. He wasn't dropped that hard. I thought about helping him up, but why? That would be too corny. Ponytail got himself up and dejectedly made his way out of the churned mud pit.

A dude twice my size came in and slammed me in less than five seconds. That shit hurt, but I didn't care. I had my one win.

I walked back to where Alexander was standing, not able to read the look on his face.

"Why didn't you help that boy up?" he asked.

"He got down there himself, so why couldn't he pick himself back up?" I shot back.

Alexander shrugged his shoulders and walked away.

I turned back to the clearing, and I saw Ponytail glaring at me. Even though one can't actually see an ego, I just knew his was crushed all to hell. Good. Stop being so damned arrogant and aggressive, then. Thor was behind him, whispering in his ear and patting him on the shoulder. Ponytail kept staring at me, so I scratched my forehead using only my middle finger. Fine, I'd cheated, but I'd still won. Even though the crowd had cheered, no one seemed to be genuinely happy with my success. My confidence and elation drained.

What really bugged me out was Alexander's reaction to the match. Did he know that I had cheated? Not that I really cared, I'd won. I was a black man in the woods surrounded by more white dudes than a black stripper, so I felt within my rights to win by any means necessary.

The rest of the afternoon passed by as waves of ideas rather than chronological events. There was talk about the matches—including mine—and there was talk about how to reconcile the modern version of God with the primal masculinity that we should all be striving for. It was heady and fascinating stuff, but as usual I acutely felt my outsider status.

The thing was I didn't know if these men were keeping me at a distance or if it was the other way around. When you have confusion about your gender and your ethnicity and your culture, it is just as easy to alienate yourself from others as it is for them to leave you out in the cold. And as I was walking around the campsite, it was impossible for me to discern which one applied.

Alexander, who was eating his lunch under an enormous tree, glanced over at me but didn't say anything further. My stomach tightened, and I figured that, because of his negative energy, I was going to have to figure out how to get back in his good graces or beat his ass, take his car, and get back home. Stepping to him in humility was out of the question. It was time to bring the street to the woods.

"What's your problem?" I asked, forcing deeper bass into my voice.

He didn't speak immediately. He finished chewing and swallowing and then, to my utter impatient anger, took another mouthful of food, chewed, and swallowed and then waited a few more seconds to give me my answer.

Patience is not something I'm known for or do particularly well.

"You embarrassed that kid today," Alexander finally said.

"What? I was supposed to lose?" I shot back.

"You could have let him keep his dignity. You could have helped him up from the ground. You could have accepted the fact that he was better than you and not have spit in his face so you could have the win. Do you even know who he is?" he countered.

I shrugged, wondering how he knew that I'd spit on old boy. Ponytail was a snitch.

"He is the son of the man who put this all together." Alexander said this as if I should have been impressed to the core of my being.

Damn, I thought to myself. I think I did know whose son he was, and I had figured out who had organized the retreat. Ponytail was Thor's son. I had whooped the leader's son. That couldn't be good.

Alexander, in full sage mode, said, "Our actions always affect more than just us. Everything we do will have repercussions for dozens of others, whether we know it or not. So by you beating that kid the way that you did, everyone who was there will have been affected by your actions. Maybe we'll start being more selective about allowing new people to attend, maybe the rules of the one-fall will be changed, and maybe some people may change the way they view and feel about young black men."

And there it was. I was wondering when the other side of the race coin was going to be flipped. I take full responsibility for my mind being in that zone. When you're black, it's hard not to think in terms of race, because your skin is the focal point for so many people's hopes, fears, dreams, and hatred. But here, I figured that my gender, my penis, would elevate me above the story of my skin. Guess not.

"So," I started, "what you're trying to tell me is that this so-called revolutionary men's movement is just as backward and racist as second-wave feminism? My singular actions would cause a group of enlightened men to demonize a whole race owing to their perceptions of one person? That's bullshit."

"It may be bullshit, but it just may be true," Alexander said, his face a little flushed. "You cheated, let another man down. That is dishonorable, not to mention that you embarrassed the son of this group's leader."

Here I was, in the middle of the goddamn woods, and I still had to experience the fragility of the male ego. When would it end? I could give a fuck about whose son had been beaten. Nor did I care about his feelings regarding what had happened. I've been in tons of fights, and whether they were serious or not, I always tried to win, no matter what. It didn't matter if it was just slap boxing in the street or a real conflict—my goal was to win. There aren't two winners in a fight. Some would argue that there weren't *any* winners in a fight, but I beg to differ. If I walk away and he doesn't, I'm putting that in the win column. I won, and damn how the other dude feels about it.

I'm not saying that I enjoy violence on some perverse level, but I do respect it for what it is and will behave accordingly. I told Alexander all of this, and he looked shaken.

"It wasn't a real violent encounter," he pleaded. "It is designed for men to have an idea of how men in the past, among indigenous peoples, created fraternity. I didn't bring you here so that you could turn this sacred space into the hood."

His words were angering me by the second. So that was his aim. To rescue the little brown dude so that his liberal streak would be appeased. I told him how offensive his words were. As I explained to him what was going on for me, I was truly proud of myself. I really wanted to hit him but tamped down that emotion and verbally expressed myself.

To be honest, I did this because I was the only brother out here and he was my ride home. But the moments that I take pride in myself are few and far between, so I decided to make this instance one of those moments.

"Violence, of any kind, is never and has never been any type of a joke or recreational activity. Old-school men play-fought to practice for war. And as a black man, I'm in enemy territory every second of my life, so I'm in a warlike mind-set all of the time."

It now became abundantly apparent that this particular men's group was trying to carve out a positive masculine existence by corrupting what had come before it. These men were taking all of these real-world lessons and emasculating them. You can't have play violence. Violence is violence, and it runs on a scale. One is an offhand harsh comment said in unthinking anger, ten a forceful shove, twenty a kick to the nuts, and so on.

This may have seemed like a negative situation, but it was just the opposite. I was learning more and more about the constructed masculine condition than I thought possible. Along this learning curve, I found out more about who I was willing and not willing to become.

These dudes in the woods were suspect. Their entire philosophy was fraudulent. They were remixing cultures to suit themselves, while I was adhering to the honesty of my circumstance. I was a hood dude trying to learn how to be a better person. These folks pretended to be forward thinking and enlightened but were just as confused as I was. They got props for investigating the question, but they were going about it the wrong way. I know that's a judgment, but there it is.

Wow! Revelations! Even though a bunch of things were becoming clearer to me, I felt rather empty. Maybe the standards I had set for my search for the authentically masculine were so grandiose that nothing would ever be able to measure up. I thought I had set the bar too high, and no matter what I did, saw, heard or experienced, all of it would fall criminally short. A lesson is a lesson.

Looking at each other, Alexander and I knew that it was time for me to get the hell out of there. We would not be camping under the stars. That suited me just fine. I was missing the concrete and steel.

Alexander felt that he had failed in his mission, and I had learned all that I was going to learn. Well, I didn't exactly learn anything. It was just confirmation that I can sometimes be a self-centered asshole, and I needed to work on that. But damn, self-centeredness is such a useful skill.

By adopting this worldview, I didn't have to take anyone else's feelings into account. I never had to get close to anyone. I never had to be vulnerable or truly accept an opposing viewpoint. I could tool around my universe with the emotional maturity of a turnip and be OK with that. It was obvious that for me to continue on my quest toward my manhood, my ego would have to be a casualty. But right then, in the woods, surrounded by people I didn't know, at the transportation mercy of a dude I met only a few days prior and being known as the black guy who spit in the leader's son's face, my ego was all I had, and it was welcome protection.

We stalked back to the campsite in a silence that was more profound than the sentient silence of the woods.

When we arrived, two older, bearded white dudes were waiting for us.

"Where were you two?" Beard #1 asked, with a twinkle in his eye that made me feel uncomfortable.

"Did you make any connections?" Beard #2 asked, smirking.

Sharply, Alexander shook his head, and the Beards seemed to be disappointed. I have no idea why these cats thought they were speaking in code. They were talking about sex! Oh, hell no. Did Alexander bring me up here thinking he was going to bugger some ghetto kid? I thought about stabbing him. Just shank him and the Beards and get out of there. Gandalf thought that he was going to turn me out in the woods. I can't describe how that made me feel. Was he going to ask, or were he and his bearded buddies going to try to gang-rape me?

Thoughts and feelings of anger and violence flooded my entire body. I was angry from the soles of my feet to the tips of my hair, and I was ready to unload it on the three dudes standing around and looking awkwardly at one another. I was shaking, I knew that, but I also felt a little of my trust for others peel off and fall away down some endless tunnel. See, this is the type of shit that happens when you step into the white world, I thought to myself.

It made me sick to think that the underlying fear and distrust that I had of white people was based in reality. I wasn't just being paranoid; this was how it was. I have revised this position several times over the course of my life, but in that place, at that time, it was the truth.

There must have been something in my eyes because the energy of the conversation shifted clumsily.

"You know you guys missed the Oath, don't you?" Beard #2 informed us.

Alexander's eyes grew wide and then closed down to narrow, nearly crying slits. He continuously shook his head and muttered to himself. I could not make out what he was saying, but it sounded like "That's the best part."

I must have looked confused, because without prompting, the Beards demonstrated the Oath.

They faced each other, stood less than an arm's distance away, and then, with their right hands, grabbed each other's dicks, over their pants—thank God. It wasn't just a little grab; they were holding on like the penis was a handlebar.

While holding each other in this way, they swore allegiance to each other in all areas of their lives: love, financial matters, personal development, and a host of other things. When they were finished, they lingered on each other's dicks a little too long, during which time Alexander's face was painted with unshielded jealousy. "It's really time to go," he said in a very small voice.

Strained could be one way to describe the drive back to my house, but silently hostile would be a bit more accurate.

Getting over the fact that I had almost had a *Deliverance* experience was nearly impossible. You'd think that Alexander would have asked if I was into men, instead of bringing me out to the wilderness in hopes of springing some homosexual trap. Intellectually, I knew that any *men's group gathering* would have a homoerotic element. Male homoeroticism is rather prevalent in American culture. Just take a look at any sporting event (including the fans) and the movies *Top Gun*, *Face/Off*, and *The Godfather* films for more on that point.

While I wasn't a big fan of homoeroticism, I knew I was going to be operating within that cultural environment. But homosexuality, especially unwarranted advances, was not even part of the equation.

I still have my conditioned negative responses to homo-sexual behavior, but as an adult I've been working hard to undo all of that. I'm trying to care less about whom people sleep with and how they do it. But it is hard.

When I was a kid, an unwanted homosexual advance was a no-no—a big one. The kind that could get you killed. I don't know what would have happened if Alexander had tried to make a pass at me. Truthfully, and I am so disgusted to reveal this, I'd likely be writing this from a cramped jail cell. I'm so glad that the events unfolded the way they did or else Alexander and I would have both been in a lot of trouble.

As I write this, and am reliving those strong emotions—almost as strong as they were when the event took place—I find myself tiptoeing around my childhood abuse, and I find that I am not yet brave enough to tackle that event in either writing or conversation. I will one day but not now. It is not something that you just *do*. Certain pains are public, while others are private. Let's just say that as a child I endured significant physical and sexual abuse.

I'm positive that my uneasiness around anything homo-sexual is directly linked with that past abuse and that I'll never be able to fully accept gay people until I deal with it—but I just can't. Just know that my strong reactions to Alexander's undeclared attempts to lure me into some homosexual act are rooted in my own prior experiences.

In the car, Alexander's face was focused on the road ahead. He wasn't looking my way for anything. I wanted to be as stonelike as he was, but I just had to know.

"What did you have in mind?" I asked him through clenched teeth, my anger barely held in check.

After several attempts of trying to say something, he finally spoke. His voice was that of a person who had found out something about himself that he really didn't like. The words spilled from his mouth like guilty molasses.

"I just thought that I'd show you a new world. You looked so lost and confused, and I felt that I could help you."

"Help me? By setting me up so that you and your buddies could force me into sex?" I tried to make each word a knife.

"It wasn't like that." His defense was halfhearted. "It was just supposed to be you and me. I would have asked, and we wouldn't have done anything that you didn't want to." Alexander was trying to convince himself. "But then when you cheated in the one-fall, I realized that you didn't deserve the gift."

Gift? Alexander was crazy as hell. "I didn't deserve to have some old white dude try to molest me? You must be out of your damn mind. Just to let you know, if you would have tried anything, you'd have been laid out in the woods somewhere, and I'd be driving your car back home."

He stiffened and drove the rest of the way in silence.

When we pulled up to my building, the whole neighborhood was out in force. Hundreds of eyes were locked on the Supra. When I stepped out of the car, people jockeyed for position to see inside. They saw Alexander crying at the wheel, and then they saw me striding triumphantly up the stairs, without a backward glance. They went back and forth like this for a while, until Alexander leaned over to shut my door and tore out of there with an earsplitting screech of tires.

I couldn't have been in a better position—reputation-wise—in the neighborhood.

They saw a white dude with a nice car pick me up earlier that day and then drop me off that evening, sobbing like a little baby. For the next few weeks, people would ask me what had happened. I never told them anything.

In projects and ghettos the world over, mystery is about as good a currency as reputation and the ability to fight or talk shit, so I kept it all to myself.

Well, that is, until I put it down on paper.

My Much Better Half

My wife, Janet, and I are not supposed to be together this long: five years—and counting—married, plus a few more "living in sin." This may not seem like such a long time, but black relationships are measured in extended time, especially for our generation. To all of our friends and associates, we've been together for almost fifty years.

The black folks of my generation are on that immediate gratification shit. To invest in a relationship takes too much time, time that could be spent in the pursuit of other partners, with whom it will take less time to do . . . whatever. Personally, I blame modern black music. Damn near every song is about hitting it on the way home from the club or cheating. Very few of our musicians are talking about courtship. But I digress.

Janet and I took our time, and we're still doing the damn thing. And people cannot stand it.

We're "that couple": the couple that most people are sickened by because of our uncanny ability—and desire—to make it work. Most of our social circle detest the fact that we're still making it happen. "You guys are always together," they hurl at us—as if that was such a bad thing. But the sentiment has to be decoded along gender lines.

When the guys say it, it should be translated as such: "Are you sure you want to sleep with the same woman for the rest of your life? I couldn't do it." The women's subliminal commentary—most of whom have one to three kids hanging off them—is: "I wish I had a man who stayed around. I have all these kids, and I'm doing this shit by myself. I hope they break up soon so that I have someone to be miserable with." Is this a generalization? Sure it is. But you'd be surprised what you hear when no one thinks you're paying attention. Well, fuck 'em. We're happy, but it's not like it didn't take a whole lot of work to get here.

We met at a poetry reading. Yep, we live in the Bay Area of California. She was a performer, and my fellow miscreants and I were in the audience heckling some of the poets. Our heckling was an act of rebellion against a scene that had shifted from alive and vibrant to dead and clichéd. People confused ill-informed political thought with revolutionary rhetoric, and we were all sick of it. All of us missed the dangerous words that brought the scene to fruition. Now that people were making money from it, all of the danger morphed into three minutes of formulaic, crowd-pleasing verse. So we clowned everyone we thought wasn't bringing it as hard as they could. We were loud and rowdy, yet infectious and soon had most of the crowd on our side. That is until I broke a chair.

My boy Naru said something that made me laugh so hard that I rocked back, lifting the chair onto its back legs. But instead of falling forward, I felt myself slowly going even farther backward. I looked down, and the legs of the chair looked like macaroni. There was a huge crack, and I landed on my back, my breath escaping in a puff of licorice root–scented embarrassment. I had obliterated the chair. Being equal opportunity assholes, my boys fell out. They all leapt to their feet and burst into laughter. Then the rest of the theater started laughing. While this was going on, my future wife was onstage waiting for the commotion to die down.

Someone helped me to my feet and gave me another chair. My bruised ego and I sat down and offered up a universal thank-you that the theater was dark. As soon as it was quiet, she spoke. Damn, her voice was deep. Catholic mass resonance poured from her tiny self. Her voice was kind of like a dude's, but I found myself oddly compelled. I wouldn't exactly call it attraction. I had more of a keen interest.

As she continued, I felt more and more drawn in. I even changed my seat so that I could see her better. Her voice, and her poetry, did not match her look.

Normally, I was attracted to fashion-forward, glamazon punk–type women—all nice clothes, five foot ten plus, and tattoos. But Janet wasn't that at all. She was little, with short hair, ethnically ambiguous, and wearing a blouse. A blouse was some shit that you wore to a job interview or to your youngest cousin's graduation. You didn't wear it to a performance.

I understand now that I was being completely shallow, but this was how I was processing the moment.

If I had to sum up how she looked, I'd have to say that she was librarian chic—very attractive and well dressed but not one to generate sexual thoughts in others. Yet when the event concluded, I found myself seeking her out. If anything, I'm recklessly confident, so I traipsed right up to her, introduced myself, and complimented her on her reading. But then, something strange happened.

When I finally stopped overwhelming her with my words, I felt my heart beat faster. Sweat trickled from the small of my back and down my ass crack. I even remember trembling a little. Was I allergic to her, or was I attracted?

She was courteous enough to make small talk. Wary, but courteous.

Aside from thinking that she was good looking, I also truly enjoyed how she performed. I asked her if she'd be willing to do a show with me and a couple of my friends. She said that she was interested and then she asked me for a business card. First a blouse, now a business card. Who was this woman?

I fumbled through my wallet—this woman was making me fiercely nervous—and then I dropped everything. Money and folded scraps of paper rained on her feet. I made some half-assed joke about not being able to find one and asked for her number. She was not having it. She asked for mine and made it really clear that she wasn't coming off one digit. I wrote it down for her, and she was off like a prom dress.

We met the next week, and she was all business. I brought her a copy of my boy's performance video, *Ebonic Plague*, and she gave me copyright forms—to ensure that the work I did was protected. She was all business and nothing but. After that we spoke every day. We spoke about her faith and my rough childhood, her being a professional roller skater and my petty theft. I wanted to share myself with her. If you met her, you'd get it. She is, hands down, one of the most trustworthy people on the planet. She gives off this vibe of caring and of being genuinely interested. You could tell her anything and know for sure that your secret was safe. I'd never encountered that before. I was almost always on my guard, even with my friends. But with her, it felt as if I had a free pass to unburden myself without consequence. And from her side, I'm sure she had never met a person who would speak freely about some of the things that I had seen and done. She told me that our conversations made her realize that the world she was in was very limited, and I showed her a whole new—albeit frightening—place. For all our talking, we didn't see each other again for almost a month. But the talking made me fall for her. How the hell do you fall in love over the telephone?

That's just what happened.

Round two found us on something more datelike. We actually went to dinner and then took a walk around Oakland's infamous Lake Merritt. (The day I moved to Oakland, I took a walk around the lake as the cops pulled two bodies out. Ten years later, I still get the chills every time I walk by that section of the lake.)

It was a pretty romantic comedyesque scene.

We were sitting on a bench, the sun was setting, kids were playing, and people looked at us and nodded, smiles on their faces. I leaned in to kiss her, but with an almost imperceptible movement of her head, my kiss landed on the side of her right eye. Touching her skin made me dizzy, and I wanted to try again, but I knew that if I did, the whole enterprise would have been shut down. The aborted lip kiss was the opening she needed to ask me to take her home. After I dropped her off, we didn't see each other for a year.

I thought about her every day.

She went off to Kansas City to live and work with some nuns. Yes, nuns. My wife is a cradle Catholic—even earning a master's degree in religion. After discovering this, our previous interactions made sense. She was virtuous in the best sense of the word. When we talked, I told her about some of my wilder adventures. Part of me wanted to show her my flaws because I was tired of carrying the weight of my dishonesty, my fears, and my pain, but the mischievous bastard side of me wanted to shock her. I wanted to see how far I could push her, see if we were going to have anything more than just a cursory friendship. She took it all, asked questions, and approached our interactions like a field study. But she always maintained her virtue, didn't take the bait. She holds her values like one would hold a newborn baby, gently but fiercely protective.

During that year, our communication consisted of lengthy e-mails and some phone calls. When she returned, all of those old feelings came rushing back. I wasn't allergic to her—I was in love. And she was as well.

We dated for a short while—no more than a year—and then we moved in together. This was a turning point for her. By moving in with me, and our being unmarried, she had turned her back on an aspect of her faith. Outwardly she was down with it, but in those moments when she thought that I wasn't looking, I could see her struggle.

To this day she has never told me how much she sacrificed—friends, respect, the goodwill of fellow parishioners, but I know and have been trying to make it up to her every day that we're together.

Cohabitating turned into getting engaged, and engagement turned into getting married. It was the most incredible day of my life, despite the fact that I had a 103-degree temperature and was getting my ass kicked by strep throat.

Against church doctrine, we were married outside, in the woods. I know I'm not the biggest fan of the outdoors, but it seemed right for us to be married among some of the tallest trees in California. If I tilted my head in just the right way, I could pretend that the trees were skyscrapers.

I don't know how she did it, but she got a friend of hers who was a priest to perform the ceremony and another friend to put it on the books as if we were married in his church. My baby has skills.

The ceremony took place within a circle of friends and family, and when our self-penned vows were uttered and rings exchanged, the circle closed in and every single person touched us. I cried so hard. I had no idea what I did to deserve her or the outpouring of love. Even in what was supposed to be one of the best moments of my life, I doubted that I deserved to be loved. Well, it could have been the fever that was causing the delusions.

When I recovered—the second day of our honeymoon—I looked at her while she was sleeping and saw the smile on her face. She was so damn beautiful. There is something so intimate about sleep. While we are asleep, we're at our most vulnerable. And for her to be able to sleep so soundly in my presence let me know that I must be doing something right. Fuck the dumb shit, I deserved this. And I still feel that way. But, of course, there had to be a hiccup.

In our seventh year of being together, we almost called it quits. Some people call it the "seven-year itch," but I call it "Get the hell away from me." We were arguing all of the time. Most of our fights were on some city-mouse/country-mouse shit. She thought that I was inconsiderate, too aggressive, and not compassionate enough (which is true), and I thought that she was way too soft. Way too sensitive and not worldly enough. And what made the arguments worse than they should have been was that she didn't know how to be mad in the moment.

Something would happen, and it would take her a week to process it. I'd be over it, but she'd just be getting started. I can't tell you how frustrating that shit was. I'd be eating my Pop-Tarts, and she'd come at me, accusing me of all sorts of stuff. It would take me a minute to register what she was going on about, and then I'd snap back at her, not trying to explain myself but trying to hurt her feelings so she'd shut up, run to the bedroom, and cry the anger out of her system. You don't do that to people you love.

We'd come to our senses, apologize, have sex, and try to get back on the righteous track. But it was habitual, not a conscious choice, so we deteriorated even more. We were rotting to the point where I was going to leave. I couldn't stand the fact that I wanted to hurt her. I also couldn't stand that she would find anything and everything to pick at. It was unhealthy and confirmed for me that black folks—no matter that each of us is only ethnically half black—were not designed to live happily ever after. And some of my so-called friends were no help.

It's very rare that I reach out for consolation, but in this case I needed help in figuring out how in the hell to salvage my marriage. Most of my boys were of no use. None of them had ever been in a relationship that lasted for more than a mosquito's life span. One of them was even a virgin in his thirties, so he was no help, for damn sure. But it was an ex-friend who said some shit that just chilled me. "Hurry up and dump her ass so that we can go and kick it like we used to." Selfish fuck. I just looked at him. This is your brain. This is your brain on warped black masculinity.

I didn't consult with any of my female friends because most of them felt that Janet and I were incompatible. Well, they thought that Janet was quite possibly out of my league. One friend described our relationship as blood and white carpet. While the blood was this raw and pure thing, it stained the carpet. And no matter how much you scrub it, the carpet will still be stained. I was the blood. Even though it is true— I do feel as if I expose her to too much—that was some cold-blooded shit to say.

Around the time of our near dissolution, a whole lot of couples in our circle were falling apart. The carcasses of spent relationships littered our social scene. It would have been so easy to just give up, lie down, and let our marriage evaporate into nothingness. But if we were willing to do that, why did we get married in the first place? Was our marriage just an extended one-night stand? Did my wife turn away from her faith for no reason? Thank everything that this was not the case. All it took for us to get right was to reconnect with what made us fall in love—each other.

We made concentrated efforts to not take each other for granted, made conscious decisions to say, "please," and "thank you." We listened to each other out of genuine love and interest, not just because it was expected of us. But the main thing that saved us was that we never stopped being curious.

If you feel as if you know everything there is to know about your partner, you might want to review your reasons for still being with that person. And the only way that we can continue to discover new shit about our lovers is by not being around them all the damn time. While some of our friends think we are conjoined, Janet and I have our own interests. She likes to hike, but I don't mess with nature. I like punk music; she'd break my CDs if she could. But when we come back together, we can share our experiences, and through the sharing it just gets better. I can say, without any sort of hesitation, that I am happily married. And the part that really sucks is that within our circle only a few can share the same claim.

Most of our friends are people of color. And within this group, all of the couples are transracial, and the pairs consisting of one black partner are worse off than the rest. Janet attributes it to black people's lacking the ability to love themselves in any full way. Being both a high school teacher and a college professor, she witnesses how young black people reinforce society's hatred of them by accepting and perpetrating every possible stereotype. Her heart breaks for these young people because she is acutely aware that they will grow up and become like some of our friends. I didn't want to agree with her at first, but as time goes on, more and more her words ring truthful. And I'm so glad that when I let my despair for my people choke me, she's around to help me get through it. With a kiss to my right eye, a shoulder rub, and a corny joke, Janet makes it a little easier to live in this world.

Babe, I want to appreciate you for putting up with—and calling me out on—my shit. Thank you for holding me accountable and for sometimes just taking a few steps back and letting me do my thing (even though it may embarrass you). I appreciate you for getting your second master's and being so humble that no one even knew that you were doing it. Thank you for allowing me to witness your transformation from processed hair to fierce locks. I appreciate you for being so willing to drop everything and help those you love. Thank you for protecting me when I need to let my ever-present guard down. I will never be able to show or say just how much I love you. But I will never stop trying.

Fear of a Black Penis

The Big Black Penis was the first weapon of mass destruction to spring up on American shores. The white comfort zone of a newly formed America was so shaken by its power that whites had no choice but to stamp it out any way they could. When we were lynched, it wasn't enough for us to dangle from tree branches; our captors had to chop off our dicks and shove them in our mouths, in effect silencing us on two different fronts. The Black Penis—rather, the mythic, ubersexual power that resided in it—destroyed an entire society's sense of decency, compassion, empathy, place, and belonging. The Black Penis was the first ICBM (Ignorant Coon's Big Machinery) the white majority ever created.

In this new America, black folks were the wild card. No matter how secure the white majority was in their dominion over us, there was always a hint that their kingdom wasn't as solid as they thought. In one sense, they had every right to be uneasy—we were too open, too free, too dark and mysterious, and just too damn beautiful for them to get a handle on.

So, instead of dealing with their own puritanical antisexuality, afraid of the *other* baggage, they had to take out their anger and confusion on our genitals. What better way to subjugate a people than to attack their most primal, pure selves? That's what they've done. From the rape of black women and physical and psychic emasculation of black men in the past to the current state of all things black and sexual—like Janet Jackson's tit—being a form of kryptonite to the smooth workings of American society. It is now time to reclaim our sexuality—not on some savage, where's-the-white-girls-at shit but on a firm, yet humble, hostile takeover.

The Black Penis does not define black masculinity, but it is its symbol; and just like America doesn't want its flag to touch the ground, we should never allow anyone to sully our national symbol. We must keep the Black Penis healthy and erect. But it is a phallic Janus. When used properly, it is a force for love and community building, but if used negatively, it is the reinforcement of every stereotype, from D. W. Griffith's *The Birth of a Nation* to the Kobe Bryant rape case and comedian Steve Harvey's uncaring and inappropriate jokes regarding the same issue. I'm going to stray a bit and remind you all what Mr. Harvey said. Apparently the woman said that her vagina was "all torn up." Steve Harvey said, and I'm paraphrasing, "Of course she was torn up. She was messing with a black man." Shit like that makes me so disgusted.

Let's get back to it.

It is high time for us to change the way that we and the rest of the world view our sexual natures. Black masculinity, including the Black Penis, is our heritage, our birthright, the force that has allowed us to press on, despite the weight of an entire society attempting to hold us back. We've made it this far, but we haven't gone far enough.

We owe it to every brother who has been beaten or killed for looking at a white girl, to every brother who showed his penis at a public urinal and was punished for it, to every brother who had his dick amputated and shoved down his throat for no reason other than white fear and hatred. We owe it to these brothers to be responsible, caring, and loving because with a Big Black Penis comes big responsibility. Use your power wisely.

Stay erect and keep your head up.

Parting Shot

So why did I write this book? It is most definitely not a scholarly work. I do not answer any questions or cite any other sources—save myself—and I use more profanity than is probably necessary. Frankly, I wrote it because I was angry, tired, fed up, and sick of sitting on the sidelines while others attempted to explain my manhood to me. After a long stretch of public silence, I felt the need to be heard.

At the turn of the century so many men are writing books and essays and appearing on talk shows to explain their versions of manhood and masculinity. Some of these takes are entertaining, some are insightful, but most are downright offensive and racially exclusive. There are even women writing to men about men, and this kind of tripped me out. Not to say that women don't have insights into the masculine mind, but if I tried to write a book about what I thought women needed to do during their menses, for example, I'd be strung up in the public square and crucified; my hands, my penis, and a broken iMac would be bolted to a pole, warning all other men not to venture where I had tread.

With all of my anger about masculinity, I thought that I should toss my little hat into the ring. The only credentials I have for addressing this topic are my life experiences as a black male. Hell, these are the only credentials I need.

For damn near all of my life, I have been investigating various forms of self-defense—physical, spiritual, and emotional—to protect myself from the burden of being a man, to insulate myself against the heavy and burning cloak of black masculinity. When I was growing up, there was nothing worse than being a black male, but on the flip side, there was nothing cooler. I'm talking about *cool* in the jazz sense of the word, not white frat-boy cool. And being cool was the world's greatest form of self-defense. By acting cool, I could be detached from everything. I could be a punk, a political and social wallflower, not committing to any cause because I was cool, and cool motherfuckers concerned themselves only with what was cool—mainly the superficial.

I was tired of being a superficial cat and felt the need to take action. This book you are holding is my biggest action to date, but there are bigger actions to come.

Lucky for all of you that gender and culture are my passions, and you will therefore be able to witness me spit my own brand of vitriol for years and years.

Don't fret; this Big Black Penis will be coming for a long, long time.